W9-BKK-589

10⁰²

1κρ

5-93

Pastors Off the Record

Stefan Ulstein

STRAIGHT TALK ABOUT LIFE IN THE MINISTRY

INTERVARSITY PRESS
DOWNERS GROVE, ILLINOIS 60515

The Library of
Chuck Sackett

© *1993 by Stefan Ulstein*

All rights reserved. No part of this book may be reproduced in any form without written permission from InterVarsity Press, P.O. Box 1400, Downers Grove, Illinois 60515.

InterVarsity Press® is the book-publishing division of InterVarsity Christian Fellowship®, a student movement active on campus at hundreds of universities, colleges and schools of nursing in the United States of America, and a member movement of the International Fellowship of Evangelical Students. For information about local and regional activities, write Public Relations Dept., InterVarsity Christian Fellowship, 6400 Schroeder Rd., P.O. Box 7895, Madison, WI 53707-7895.

Cover photograph: Michael Goss

ISBN 0-8308-1346-2

Printed in the United States of America ∞

Library of Congress Cataloging-in-Publication Data

Ulstein, Stefan.
*   Pastors off the record: straight talk about life in the ministry*
*   /Stefan Ulstein.*
*   p.   cm.*
*   ISBN 0-8308-1346-2*
*   1. Clergy—Office.   2. Clergy—United States—Interviews.*
3. Clergy—Canada—Interviews.   I. Title.
BV660.2.U58   1993
253'.2—dc20   *93-7398*
                                                              CIP

17	16	15	14	13	12	11	10	9	8	7	6	5	4	3	2	1
07	06	05	04	03	02	01	00	99	98	97	96	95	94	93		

*In memory of Hank Weston,
who always went after
the sheep that was lost.*

Acknowledgments

This book would not have been possible without the encouragement and support of many good friends. Professor Henry Baron invited me to the excellent Christian Writers in Community Conference at Calvin College, where I met my editor, Rodney Clapp. Rodney listened to the germ of my idea, helped me to focus it into a workable project and guided me to the finish line.

Psychologist Brian Whitney of Bellevue Community Services met with me early on to discuss the psychological aspects of the pastorate and to suggest constructive ways to frame my questions.

Seattle film publicist Nancy Locke, who over the years has introduced me to many filmmakers, gave me the opportunity to develop the interviewer's craft.

Chuck Pasma and Bill Safstrom, superintendent and principal at Bellevue Christian School, have backed me all the way, providing time off to travel, interview and write when deadlines approached.

The scores of pastors who graciously met with me were a real inspiration. Some of their voices speak in these pages; others echo in the background, having served to frame and clarify the issues.

But none of this would have happened without my wife, Jeanne, who led me to Christ when we were just kids, inspired me to get an education and enriched my life in countless ways.

Introduction

My interest in talking to pastors "off the record" began a quarter-century ago, not too long after I became a Christian. My conversion, at the age of eighteen, was of the Damascus Road variety. Old friends were shocked by the changes in my life. A couple of Christian acquaintances confessed that they'd never expected me to become a Christian and had therefore never seriously prayed for my conversion.

My new life in Christ was a liberating, humanizing experience that came about in part because my girlfriend had given me a modern-language New Testament. Being an avid reader, I began at the beginning and read it through in a week or so. After accepting Christ, I reread it several times.

What I read, particularly in the words of Christ, was fresh, challenging and alive. If this was Christianity, I wanted more, so inevitably I began thinking about becoming a pastor. After all, I loved reading the Bible, I enjoyed being around Christian people, and I liked going to church. Why not enter a profession that would allow me to do the things I liked most? It seemed to me that the pastors I knew had the best possible life—they read the Bible, prayed, counseled and preached the good news.

Because I was in the Navy at the time, my travels took me to churches all over the United States and Asia. As I met pastors of many denominations, I watched them carefully to see what kind of people they were. I soon began to notice that pastors were somehow different from other Christians. Many of them seemed to be "on" all the time. I began to detect a professional distance between pastors and their flocks that seemed out of sync with the humanizing, freeing unity that I had found in Christ.

I gradually abandoned my plans to become a pastor and eventually ended up as an English teacher in a Christian high school—a job that put me in contact with scores of pastors, since our school draws students from over 150 churches.

I liked most of the pastors I met over the years, but I found it difficult to get close to many of them. At first I thought this was elitism on their part. *Perhaps,* I decided, *they consider themselves more holy than the rest of us.* As I got to know them better I began to hear some of the frustrations, and even cruelties, that many of them had endured, and I sensed that the professional distance was at least in part a defense mechanism.

I began to see that pastors are too often forced to wear masks not of their own choosing, and that the longer they wear them, the more they grow to fit their faces. I wondered if pastors knew this when they entered the ministry, or if it was something that crept up on them. I also wanted to know how some pastors were able to avoid wearing the mask.

I wanted to look under the clerical collar to find the person. I couldn't believe that most pastors want to be put up on a pedestal, or that most parishioners want them there. Nor could I believe that Christians in the pews want their pastors to be overextended, professionally insecure and emotionally isolated.

As I embarked upon the interviews for *Pastors Off the Record,* I wasn't sure what I'd find. I interviewed pastors from a wide range of denominations, from Canada to Mexico.

Some were in unusual ministries. I spoke to prison and military chaplains, a Korean pastor of a white Canadian church and an American pastor of a poor Mexican church.

But most of the pastors who speak their hearts in this book work in medium-sized churches in mainline, evangelical and charismatic denominations. They are demographically unremarkable—like the pastors of the churches most of us attend. The smallest congregation was under forty. The largest was over six thousand.

I wanted to find the common threads that run through the pastoral experience, regardless of the denomination or size of the church. I wanted to talk to pastors candidly about the personal side of the job— the things that they couldn't always speak openly about to their congregations.

As I began seeking interviews, some pastors could not, or would not, make time to see me, but most were gracious and eager to talk. Almost all of them were highly enthusiastic about the idea of the book. Some felt that it was long overdue and should be read by seminary students. Others hoped that if it lived up to its thematic promise, it would be widely read by churchgoers. Most believed that reading other pastors' stories would be helpful and therapeutic to pastors.

I allowed the pastors to talk off the record because I wanted them to feel free to speak their hearts. I have edited out the chitchat of our conversations along with the inevitable ums, ahs and pauses; in some cases, I've reorganized the narrative line for clarity. I chose to keep the interviews anonymous and the locations and denominations vague, so that readers could concentrate on the stories rather than the storytellers.

It is my hope that the stories of everyday pastors contained in *Pastors Off the Record* will help pastors and their congregations to break through the walls of professional expectation, careerism and petty politics that keep the church from being all that it can be in Christ.

Part 1

Personal Stress

The Meter
Is Always Running

1

He's a dapper, energetic senior pastor of a thriving church in an upscale community. When he took the pastorate here it was a small, somewhat ethnic church with a core of families who knew each other intimately. As the community changed and grew over the following two decades, so did the church. The boxy little sanctuary was replaced several years ago with a new, architecturally stylish complex. It's right downtown, a highly visible fixture in the community.

He runs his days like an executive. Years ago he was the entire staff. Now he supervises several associates. I wait in the lobby while his secretary informs him that I've arrived.

His office is tasteful, almost elegant, but unpretentious. We chat, I explain the book and we're off.

*　　　*　　　*

*T*he meter is always running. People say, "I know you're busy, I know I should call, but ..." If I go to a ball game or a party, they try to sneak in a counseling session. It's hard to put people off, but some people misuse the friendship. They know that if they call the office they might not get in for two weeks, so they try to just squeeze in.

In seminary the advice we got from older pastors was to have friends from another church. Ostensibly, the reason was to avoid jealousy, but looking back, I think they were also saying that otherwise you wouldn't get any off-duty time.

The bottom line is that you listen. You can try to change the subject, but you want to avoid looking like you're only compassionate during business hours. I've gone to a ball game with someone and been so tied up in an informal counseling session that I had to read the paper the next day to find out what went on at the game. If that happens, I make sure never to go out with that couple again.

Sometimes it's new people who just don't know how to work the system. With a lawyer or doctor you are paying them directly, so you feel empowered to just call up and ask for an appointment. Sometimes new Christians feel odd calling up and asking for an appointment when they're not directly paying for it.

In a church like this one, which was once small and intimate but is now quite large, old-timers will sometimes corner you on off-hours. In the old days they could just come by and you'd set aside whatever was on your desk and talk to them. Nowadays they come by and see the "busy" sign on the door and realize that my secretary would have to fit them into a tight, booked-up schedule. So they catch me at the coffee shop. *He laughs.* They look for my car and then come in while I'm reading the paper.

The end result is emotional exhaustion. I now literally leave town to get some quiet time. My wife and I went to a friend's cabin for three days so I could do my book work. I left my number with my son and with the senior deacon, and I told them both the same thing: If you call, it had better be so serious that it breaks my heart.

Last Sunday I got to church at 6:30 a.m. and preached three sermons back to back. Then I ducked out early, without even doing my PR thing in the foyer, because I had a couple whose marriage was in flames. I worked with them until 2:30, and that was just to keep them from physically injuring one another. We never did get to real communication.

Then I got a phone call from a forty-year-old who was attempting suicide. He just kept saying, "I'm so sorry. I'm so sorry." It took twenty minutes for me to figure out who it was, he was so upset. After forty minutes on the phone I got him to give me the phone number and I had a reverse trace put on it. We got the ambulance out there;

they brought him to the hospital and pumped his stomach. He was in a coma for a while, but by 11:00 that night the doctors figured he'd live, and I was able to get home.

Before I got there the emergency-room nurses were trying to figure out who he was, since he wasn't carrying any ID. He had a phone book, so they just started calling the numbers, trying to find out his name. Naturally, those people then called me to let me know. I got the last of those calls at 12:30 in the morning.

Then came Monday: my day off. I slept in until 8:00 and went down to my workshop. I asked my wife to tell callers that I was working. By noon I had three calls, two of which I figured I ought to return. After lunch I went to Sears and got a work stand, and as I was assembling it I got a call from a parishioner who drives the aid car. He told me that he'd just rushed the baby of another parish couple to the hospital.

I headed for the hospital. The baby died at 5:00 p.m., and I was with the parents all night. Thursday is my day to study and prepare my sermon, but that's when the memorial service was for that baby.

The next four Monday evenings are taken up with counselor training for the Billy Graham crusade, so I won't have a day and an evening off together for at least another month. So you can see that when I go to a party or a ball game, I need some off-duty time. I need an emotional sabbath. Illness, suicide, death: things like that are vitally important, so of course I drop what I'm doing. I do it gladly. But there are things that can wait, too, so I appreciate it when the nonurgent needs can be scheduled more flexibly.

Sure, I get irritated. Sometimes I get mad, but I care about these people. The thing is, they all say, "I know you're busy, or I know I should call at the office, but . . ." Everybody is making an exception to the way they usually act. If they knew how many exceptions there were, they wouldn't do it.

My wife and I have two or three couples that we really click with, that we like to do things with. They respect our off-duty time and don't try to sneak in a counseling appointment. There are other couples we really like but who can't understand that, so we just don't do things with them.

Sometimes I'll just say, "I'd really like to talk to you about this, but not now." I pull out my DayTimer and schedule an appointment right then.

*　　*　　*

My granddad was a preacher, but not my dad. The only price my dad ever paid for being a PK (preacher's kid) was a financial one. Granddad tried to make ends meet by farming, but he knew nothing about farming and they were always broke. But he was called to preach in that community, and the only way to make ends meet was to try farming.

They nearly killed all the animals on that place. My dad and his brothers once dropped a cat from the hayloft onto a horse that was trotting out of the barn. The cat landed on the horse's back and dug in its claws to get a hold. The horse took off and knocked down half the fences on the place.

Another time they had a bull that needed a ring put in its nose. The vet probably charged two or three dollars back then, but the boys figured they could save the money. They took every rope they owned and tied that bull down in his stall. Tied him over and over. Then they set to work on his nose with a leather awl and a pocketknife.

Grandpa was driving home, and he heard that bull hollering a mile down the road. When he rounded the bend, he saw his barn shaking and shimmying. The bull just about wrecked the barn, and it cost a lot of money to have the vet fix up the damage on the nose.

But although he wasn't a pastor, my dad held the ministry in a high regard. Grandpa never made any money, but he raised his kids right. Having a minister for a father ought to be a great asset, not a liability. But when I was a kid I couldn't believe all the anger some PKs had against their fathers, against the church and against God.

One of my best pals was a PK. He was on a party line, and whenever the phone rang people would eavesdrop on one another. When the preacher's ring sounded, they would all pick up just to hear what was going on. Once I called him in the morning and he said, "You're sober already? After all we had to drink last night?"

Of course we hadn't been near any booze, but he said it to get a rise out of people. It worked, too. His dad almost lost his church over that kid's antics.

*   *   *

I didn't want to use a double standard in raising my own kids. Back at our first church, when the kids were little, they were the darlings of the congregation. One was three, the other was five. Ladies would knit and sew little outfits for them. Some of the gifts were pretty garish. They were awful things. But they came from the heart.

Shortly after we came down here, my son's bike was stolen from the garage. He was really broken up about it. I filed for homeowner's insurance reimbursement, but a couple of days later he got a letter. It said, "God told me that someone needed your bike more than you did. But it's too bad that person chose to steal your bike." In the envelope was eighty dollars. We went out and got a bike that day.

A couple of weeks later we got the insurance money. My son said, "What's this for?" I told him that the money was his to use as he saw fit. We spent quite a while talking about what he could do with it— buy candy, save it for college, buy toys.

The next Sunday a parishioner brought my son to me between services. The boy was crying. The parishioner said, "I caught him coloring in the spaces on the building plan giving graph, and him being the pastor's son I thought I should put a stop to it."

My son said, "I only colored in eighty dollars' worth. I thought I was supposed to."

I told the fellow that I was going to make a statement about my kids at the second service and that I'd like him to be there since he had precipitated it. I told the congregation that my kids were normal kids and that I wanted to raise them as normal kids. I said: "I am the pastor of this church. My wife and my children are not the pastors of this church. My children are normal children, and I want to raise them as normal children. And if any one of you ever comes to me with a criticism of my kids and says, 'After all, they are the pastor's kids,' I'll nail you to the wall. I will not have my kids growing up to hate my job or my God." They all applauded, and it was never a problem.

I asked my son, who is now in the ministry himself, what he felt the cost had been growing up a preacher's kid. He said that the only downside had been that when he was growing up his friends never gave him credit for making any tough decisions. When they wanted to get drunk or take drugs and he declined, they said it was because his old man was a preacher.

But he said the upside was much greater. He got to go to Greece and Israel on tours his dad led. He got to shake hands with Billy Graham. And he got to grow up surrounded by a lot of really fine friends.

*   *   *

My wife tells me that she specifically remembers, at age fourteen, dedicating her life to becoming a pastor's wife. I didn't know that when I started dating her. It would have scared me to death, because I had no intention of becoming a pastor. She loves it though. She remembers everybody's name and phone number. She can call people and organize them.

But I think that feeling a call to be a pastor's wife may be a generational thing. It also has to do with the wife's personality and the pastor's job description.

My younger colleagues tell me that interview committees still ask, "Does your wife play the piano?" *Again, he laughs.* One guy replied, "Why yes. Would you like to interview her for a job also?" In the old days it was just sort of expected.

Nowadays wives have their own careers. I know women who get very active in their husbands' churches; I know wives who sing in the choir because they like to sing, but don't do anything else. I even know one guy whose wife only attends every other week or so.

My wife wrote an article about the joy she took from being a pastor's wife. She got a lot of letters—some positive, some negative.

One letter was downright bitter. When we were in that city on business, we looked the woman up. She was just miserable being a pastor's wife. Her husband was a pleaser. He couldn't say no to the church, so his marriage was almost on the rocks because of it.

Like a Diesel Engine Without a Governor

2

He's fifty years old but looks at least ten years younger, with the kind of pumped-up physique that men in their twenties would pay big money for at a Nautilus club. It's the kind of body that comes from either hard work or a narcissistic workout regimen. His came with his latest job. Since leaving the pulpit several years ago he's worked as a longshoreman in a busy seaport.

He left the professional ministry when he realized that his junior-high-aged daughters were growing up without a father. He still counsels people at the church where he last pastored, and he has a "tentmaking" ministry on the docks

*　　　*　　　*

I'm finally getting to do what I thought I'd be doing as a pastor. I counsel people, I lead guys at work to the Lord, and I disciple them. At night I can actually sit down in my study and read.

As a pastor, I was too busy with meetings and administration. I was like a diesel engine without a governor. The faster I went, the faster I went. I got busier and busier, and my family was left out in the cold.

Part of it had to do with the structure of the churches I served in. The pastor was expected to start new programs. The problem was that once the new programs were started, they needed someone to run the programs. If you did a good job they said, "Hey! That's great! Let's have more of that!" There wasn't a mechanism for telling the pastor to stop, or at least to slow down.

I have a different perspective on things after seeing churches operate from the inside. Thirty years ago I had strong doctrinal reasons for wanting complete local control. I didn't want to have to explain from the pulpit some trendy new move from the headquarters back East. I still have a problem with that, but I can also understand the advantages to being accountable to some organization that's larger than the local body.

The first church I pastored was really a Sunday school that had become a church. It was in a little rural community way out in the boondocks. It was just a little country church, and they wanted a part-time pastor because they didn't think they could afford a full-time guy.

They had no background as a church, so I conformed them to the Baptist mode: eleven a.m. worship, Sunday-night service, Wednesday prayer meeting. They wanted what they'd grown up with. I was in my early twenties, and that was pretty much what I knew, so away we went.

Those were the best days I ever had as a pastor. Since I was part-time I had to work, so I worked in the grocery store.

As a pastor I helped people. Helped them with the milking. If a guy had a heart attack, I'd help work his farm while he was getting better. I might help someone level a field or bring in hay.

I got to know those people very well, and we had some great conversations over the fence or in the milking parlor.

What I did in the pulpit was pretty standard fare. I preached a trust in the Word. But what really touched people was having a pastor who could empathize with them. I was part of their daily life. There wasn't that false barrier between us.

Some pastors say that the barrier grows up over time. Did you deliberately try to avoid that?

I was just twenty-three. All these farmers had milk cows, beets, corn. They were pretty well established, while I was a kid really, just out of Bible school.

One of the deacons took me out to the cow pasture and asked me,

"What do you see?"

"Cows," I said.

"No," he said, "I mean what do you see on the ground?"

"Well . . . manure, I guess."

He shook his head and sighed. "That's what I thought. You're so green you wouldn't say *shit* if you had a mouthful. Out here we call it what it is. You should learn to call things what they are, too."

That was his way of telling me not to be superficially different from the congregation. So many times over the years, when I've had to be brutally honest, I've thought of that conversation. Just call it what it is.

I tried to remain transparent. I was the pastor, but I didn't want to be some phony image. I couldn't be transparent in the pulpit, though. I felt I had to protect the integrity of the Word. I was probably the only person in town who even had a suit. My one concession was that I did wear cowboy boots with my preaching suit.

Those were neat times! I was with people when they started their families. I cried with them when they were hurting. They'd come to me for answers, and sometimes I'd just have to say, "I don't have a clue. Ask me about the Bible, though." And we'd go to the Word. It was okay that I didn't have all the answers. We searched together.

There was a lot of culture shock and moral wrestling, though. It wasn't just a walk in the pasture. There were murders sometimes, where the sheriff, the justice of the peace and basically the whole town were in cahoots.

If somebody was stealing cattle, the word would get out who the culprit was. Then it was made known that the cattle had better find their way home. Usually they did. But if they didn't, the rustler would have a hunting accident. It was a range mentality that I wasn't raised with. I grew up in the city, and you didn't just go out and shoot somebody for stealing your calves. But out there, stealing someone's livelihood was a life-and-death thing.

There were cases where somebody sexually abused a child, and they had a hunting accident too. I remember the sheriff telling me, "Nobody saw what happened out there. If they did, they'd say it was a hunting accident. So that's what it is. A hunting accident."

The justice of the peace was an old army veteran, and she had a mouth that would fry bacon. She took the same view as the sheriff.

How did you react to this range justice? Did you confront them about it?

Sure. But nobody knew who actually did the shooting. It was their way of doing things. I could have made a big, one-issue ministry, and then I'd have been shut out. I did what I could. I'm sure I'd have handled it differently if I had been older and more experienced.

I was not the big authority. I was one of them. I didn't realize at the time how much was going on. I was young, and new to the town. Maybe that's partly why I was able to be so close to those people. I knew my place and didn't try to be the big authority on every last thing. Sometimes pastors think they are the ultimate authority, but they're not. I've been back and met those people's kids and grandkids. I don't think they remember one sermon I preached, but they remember things we talked and prayed about when we were hunting, or when one of us pulled the other's car out of a snow bank.

Why did you leave that pastorate if you felt so fulfilled there?

I felt called to move to a struggling church in another town. I thought I had something to offer them, something to say. I'd had enough time in the Word to believe that biblical principles worked.

I was way too naive. I had no clue. My new ministry was a typical Bible church. Very fundamental, but not much fun. They were having real struggles, and I thought I knew how to fix the problems.

I wasn't sure that I was supposed to leave my country church, though, so when I candidated I deliberately gave them the wrong answers to their questions. I figured I knew what I was supposed to answer, but I just answered straight from the heart.

Then they told me they wanted me. They liked the way I gave them the wrong answers!

I told the country church that I'd been called, but that I wasn't sure my work with them was finished. I'd felt that I should stay until they could call a full-time pastor. So I told them that if they could call a full-time pastor I'd move on.

The deacons thought it over, and then each one said okay. They'd been thinking about it for a while, and one said he'd donate two head of cattle. Another said he'd give a quarter of a section. They secured enough to bring in a full-time pastor, so the Lord shut all the doors behind me.

So how did it go at the new church?

At first it went great. They'd had about 12 people coming to evening service, and soon it was up to 90. Morning worship went from 40 to 120 to 200.

Everybody was happy. It was great except for one little thing. I got mixed up in the idea that I had to meet their expectations. They burned me to a crisp. I had to dot every *i* and cross every *t* because someone might leave if I did anything wrong. The success was a curse. I felt that the growth was because of me and therefore it could fail because of me too.

One day, about five years later (I remember this as clearly as if it were yesterday), I looked into my mirror and blurted out, "Who are you? There's nothing about you that's just you anymore."

Did you know then that you'd have to make some big changes?

Yes and no. I decided to get back to basics. I called a board meeting and laid it out. We needed a biblical form of church government. Majority rule is simply not the biblical norm. It always boils down to "Let's throw a rock at the senior pastor and see if he bleeds."

I told them that I no longer had any interest in meeting all their expectations. If I said no to something they asked of me, then there was not a chance. I was a dry well. My ministry had been I-centered, and God was not glorified.

I could fake it. I can still take ten minutes with a Bible and a concordance and come up with a "good" sermon. But it doesn't come from my soul. It just fills up the time. I needed to get back to those "over-the-fence" conversations. It was all too packaged and managed.

I got back to my own devotional life, my family and my personal walk. Then I took a stronger stand on Christian education and really alienated some people. For a lot of fundamentalists, the public schools are God-ordained. You send your kids there to be a witness. Right!

I was a philosophy major in college, and I knew that the public schools were indoctrinating kids with a lot of values that conflicted with the Word. Then I found a Christian school that wasn't just a segregation academy, and I got very enthusiastic.

I had taken in a foster son. His father was from the little community where I had pastored before. His wife left him because of his drinking, and his life was all torn up. He was going to dry out, get a job and send for the boys.

The sixteen-year-old was bad news. He got thrown in jail for theft; then he broke out of custody when he was being transported. The guy he broke out with got shot. They caught him and put him in prison, where he got stabbed. I don't know where he is now.

The fourteen-year-old was headed in the same direction, and I knew public school would just not work for him. I put him in the Christian school. I was so impressed with its philosophy that I put my kids in too.

Well, that was a tension point in the church. A number of people left over that. Then I got honest about some other issues. I said that the pulpit wasn't just for soul-winning. They wanted to bring people to church so I could evangelize them. I told them that was their job. My job was to pastor the congregation, so I refocused my preaching from evangelization to exhortation. Not a popular move. They also balked at my statements about missions.

Now that I wasn't trying to please people, we did lose members. Things got pretty tense, and I got isolated. Then I made a big mistake that led to my leaving the pulpit.

My marriage had become pretty routine. My wife and I just weren't depending on one another anymore. We did go away together and try to make a new start, but it was me trying to fix things, not us trying to get close again.

My vanity, coupled with my anger and my chronic fatigue, led me to get closer to a woman I was counseling than I should have. It was unbiblical and unprofessional. We didn't commit adultery, if by adultery you mean sex, but I was allowing her to be my intimate, and I was giving her a part of me that belonged to my wife.

I had never before allowed myself to become close to a counselee like that. I always shared everything only with my wife. But my wife and I had ceased being lovers and confidants. We were just Mom and Dad. So I let things develop into a classical codependency.

I knew that this woman had problems fantasizing, but I was so vain and so isolated that I just figured I could handle it. When she told people in the church about our relationship, it came out quite different from what had actually happened.

How did this affect your relationship with your wife?

I was very humbled, so I was able to slow down and listen to her. Now we are closer than ever before.

It's too bad that you felt you had to step down from the pulpit. Don't you think you've gained insights that you could share as a pastor?

Maybe. But even though things got straightened out, I lost my testimony. If you're going to be a pastor, you have to be above reproach. You can't have people harboring ideas that you're a womanizer or an adulterer.

Every two years we had an internal audit at the church. We asked tough questions about ourselves and the programs. Sometimes people would mention a concern about my relationships with different women in the church. That wouldn't have happened if they didn't know about my history. So rather than leave everyone guessing, I stepped down.

I wish sometimes that I could go back and enter the ministry knowing what I know now. I remember during the really hectic times people saying, "Boy, he's some pastor! He's really done a work!"

I did, in a sense. We were kicking butt and taking names! Lots of kids were going on to Bible school, and the church looked like it was on fire. But meanwhile I was going nuts. Like I said, they burned me to a crisp.

When it fell apart I got mad at everyone except the right person: me. The relationship with the woman was just the last straw; I was headed for the skids long before.

Now I'm not an elder, or a deacon, or an anything. I'm just a guy who works in the church. I can say, "Watch me and see how I'm doing," but I'm not up there on the pastoral pedestal dodging rocks.

I wouldn't want to be an elder or a pastor in any church this side of the Mississippi. It seems that everybody in a five-state radius knows about what happened to my ministry, and they all have an opinion. It will always be there. But I do help out with counseling, budgeting, building and all sorts of things. And I get to witness, disciple and counsel guys at work, which is more like the over-the-fence ministry I started out in.

Do the other longshoremen at work know that you're an ordained minister?

They know that I counsel people. I counsel a lot of them for drug, alcohol and family things. There are a lot of people out there who have spent years of their lives and thousands of dollars on so-called counseling. They're hooked on counseling. I don't go over and over their childhood with them. After fifteen or twenty minutes I can usually tell that what they're sharing with me isn't the real problem. Since I'm not charging a fee, I can just cut to the real issue. They can't fire me.

I think I have a gift for getting to the real issue. So lots of guys refer other guys to me. Once the management even asked me to do some counseling.

There was this guy, a real redneck, who was the worst user in the world. He'd always talk about women, blacks, his fellow workers in the most disparaging terms. But he could also turn on the charm. He could make you feel that he really liked *you*, when he had nothing but venom for the rest of the human race.

When his girlfriend kicked him out, one of the guys let him stay at his place. They worked different shifts, and the redneck raped the guy's wife. He'd say he seduced her. He kept her quiet by saying that he'd tell her husband it was her idea. A real scum.

One night the husband came to work all hysterical, waving a gun and yelling, "You raped my wife! You raped my wife!" Six of us jumped him and wrestled the gun away. It was a good thing, too, because he would have killed that redneck in a second. Then he'd have gone to prison, which would have been a tragedy.

One of the guys got rid of the gun so that management wouldn't have to fire the guy. But the husband was distraught, so management asked if I'd counsel him. They were afraid he'd kill either the redneck or himself. We spent some time together, and he got a grip on things. He hasn't come to the Lord yet, but I'm not giving up on him.

The docks are kind of like that little country town I started out in. You call things by their name, and if you're straight, you'll get a hearing.

I've learned not to use God talk on these guys, because too many of them have an ax to grind with the organized church. I don't quote Scripture, either. I talk about scriptural principles without calling them that.

One guy, who was very anti-Christianity, told me that I had talked more sense to him than all of his recovery-program therapists combined. He kept telling me this, and I kept counseling with him until he'd really made some progress.

One day he finally asked, "Where do you come up with all this stuff? It really works."

I laughed and told him: It's in the Bible.

I Felt My
Life Had Been
Thirty-two Years
of Fraud

3

He's a respected school administrator in a medium-sized town. As a young man he was a rising star in his conservative denomination: an accomplished preacher, teacher and radio personality.

At thirty-two he had a nervous breakdown that led to a crisis in faith. For several years he was unable to enter a church. We meet in his office at the school district headquarters.

*   *   *

I was so young and green in those days! My wife and I both. I think about the idea of a young fellow like me being given so much responsibility, and I just shudder. I jumped on a fast track that began with college and kept going.

I spent ten years at my college. After I received my undergraduate degree and my M.A., I stayed on for my Ph.D. I taught in the college—Greek and New Testament—and I also was a radio announcer. I wrote scripts, traveled a lot on speaking engagements—my whole life was just go, go, go! And I loved every minute of it.

When it was time to move out into a regular church ministry, a friend gave my name to a search committee in Idaho. I interviewed, and it seemed like a perfect match. I just drove down there and was hired. It was a smooth transition.

It seemed that life was really great. Here we were, newlyweds, living in a nice four-bedroom, two-bath parsonage. At that point it was going the way it was supposed to.

I'd been raised in a solid evangelical church, and Christianity had just been a constant in my life for as long as I could remember. I never knew any other way of looking at things.

I plunged into my work with real enthusiasm. I'd work mentally on my sermon all week, writing things down on 5x8 cards. On Sunday morning I'd go to a café for breakfast and put the notes together in final form for that day's sermon. It was a three- or four-hour ritual that I had each week.

I was sitting in the restaurant one morning, and all of a sudden I just started to cry. It was like somebody had lowered a black curtain. I felt my life had been thirty-two years of fraud. I remember leaving the money on the counter and walking out. The crazy thing is, I still preached my sermon that morning.

That was in early December, and it started a series of events. I just couldn't shake the terrible depression. One of the deacons knew something was wrong, and he asked someone to preach for me one Sunday. He told me to take a month off and rest up. I had a good relationship with him.

I drove to a different state, to a town where I had some friends and family, and I felt better right away. A week earlier I had been literally sitting in a corner sobbing. But things looked better after being away, and I went back. It only lasted two months.

One evening I had the blackest depression. I was clinically depressed. I couldn't sleep, and I was dysfunctional in just about every area. I was still preaching and doing my job, but now I can't remember much about my ministry and preaching during that time. It must have been pretty hollow.

I had to nap all the time. My emotions were haywire. I'd get in a panic for no reason and start yelling at my wife. I don't know how either of us survived those last six months in the pulpit.

I went to a Christian doctor I knew, and we prayed together. We talked for about two hours, and then he said, "You have to leave. You're young, you have no kids. You need to leave and just start a new life doing something else."

I thought he meant a leave of absence, but he said no. He said, "It took you fifteen years to get to this point. You'll need at least three years to recuperate."

I felt so guilty. I'd been a believer since I was nine years old. I just got on the track and went to Sunday school, college, all the way to my Ph.D. I was a Bible scholar and a radio personality. This was my whole life. My whole identity. I couldn't imagine just walking away, but I knew that I couldn't stay.

The doctor told me to think of it as a temporary retreat from the battlefield. He offered to meet with the deacon board. He said that if they really cared, they'd make it easy for me to leave.

I preached one more sermon; I think it was the best sermon I ever preached. And then I packed up and left. An old deacon, who was a spiritual father to me, told me to be sure not to do anything in the next few months that I'd regret. He talked to me about Hebrews 3:12: Don't depart from the way of the Lord.

I know what he was talking about. There were four of us in our conservative denomination who pastored in that valley. All of us left the ministry within a two-year period. Two of the guys divorced their wives.

The day we left is still one of the most vivid memories of my life. We pulled out towing a trailer and just left everything behind. When we got to Pendleton, Oregon, we checked into a motel and dropped from exhaustion.

My doctor friend had given me a complete physical exam, and he told me that I was physically and emotionally empty. I guess when you're young you can abuse yourself physically without really knowing it. He told me that I wouldn't be able to get control of my mind until I was restored physically.

My wife called Hank, the man I'd worked for during college

summers, and asked if he could give me a temporary job when we got into town. Then we knelt by the bed and prayed. I was really terrified.

I thought I heard the Lord speak to me. I can't even remember the words now, but it was an audible voice that came from the cold-air vent. Your mind plays some bizarre games with you when you're sick. That was a rough night.

When we crossed the Columbia River the next day, I looked over the valley and realized that I'd never be able to go back to the ministry. Everything had changed. I just knew it clearly and absolutely in that moment.

* * *

In my mind I've gone back over my time in the ministry a thousand times. I was physically exhausted, yet I loved every minute of it. We started a young mothers' fellowship when we began our ministry in the church. That went well so we started a parenting group. That grew to fifty couples and became the core group of the church.

The membership expanded, and soon I had something every night—church meetings, fellowships, prayer meetings, speaking engagements. I had a radio broadcast live at 7:30 each morning. At that age you think you're invincible. Sometimes I'd be in my office, and I'd just put my head down and fall right asleep. It was constant stress with no time to unwind. I was always going and, at the same time, planning my radio talks and my sermon.

When it fell apart, it was like a house of cards. It was that quick. Then it was three years before I could even go into a church.

* * *

I think my upbringing had something to do with it. I grew up in a rigid fundamentalist system that oversimplified everything: When you're lonely, do this. If you're in pain, do that. If things haven't worked out, it's because you lack faith.

But out in the homes I saw people get divorced. I saw families that were driving their children crazy. I'd pray for a person to get well and then they'd die.

I never knew what faith was. I knew a system of things that was supposed to fix what was wrong. I'd never considered any alternative way to look at things. My way was the right way.

My college years confirmed me in that way of thinking. In college I was very academic—as a student and graduate student, and then as a teacher. Staying in that one school setting, where we were taught that we had all the answers, was part of my problem. I taught Old Testament, New Testament, languages, the whole schmeer. But I never allowed myself to question. I had a utopian vision of what the church and the faith were. I had all the answers.

But when I began to pastor, I saw things work out much differently than they were supposed to. I went to a pastors' conference and saw bitter fighting between the San Francisco and Denver seminary groups. The seminaries were considered part of the denomination, and it was awful to see the fighting. At meetings I'd watch as pastors talked about ways to control the elections, as though they were members of a union or a political party.

My faith had been held together by a system, and when I became disillusioned with the system I became agnostic. I had no idea what I believed. I'd thought that I was examining truth, but really I'd just accepted as truth all the things I'd been taught. Then I'd taught them to other people as the truth.

*   *   *

So I went back to working with Hank, who was a Japanese-American landscape gardener. Hank was a deacon in his Baptist church and a very active Christian, but he was the first person in all that time who didn't try to "fix it."

Almost everybody had some solution for me. There was sin in my life. Do this. Do that. Somebody gave me a handkerchief they'd prayed on. Hank just accepted me without trying to fix it. We worked together every day, and he was just there for me. Solid. Loving. But without trying to make it go away.

I was feeling so much guilt. I remember so vividly that feeling of failure. I just couldn't hear when people had a solution. Hank knew that. He was so wise. He could be with a person and provide strength and encouragement, but he didn't try to take control.

I felt so awful about letting everyone down that I was paralyzed by guilt and failure. I couldn't stand to face people. Hank told me that the people who cared about me would understand what I was going through, and the ones who didn't weren't my friends anyway.

Hank kept me from sinking any deeper. He was the wisest, most loving Christian man I've ever met. We'd work together, go fishing, but he was wise enough not to push me.

Why do you think Hank was able to understand your needs when others couldn't?

Maybe it was because of all he'd been through. He was an American citizen and an army vet, but when World War II came along he'd had to leave town or go into a relocation camp because his folks had come from Japan. He lost his farms and was treated like an enemy alien. When the war was over, he faced a lot of discrimination, but he never let it get him down. He saw the long view.

I'll tell you a story about him that will give you an idea about his composure. We were fly-fishing up in Canada, and a hook went through his eyelid. Right through! I don't quite understand the Asian double eyelid—I think there's an extra fold of skin or something—but it didn't touch his eye. Anyway—*he laughs*—he said that fishing was too good for us to leave, so he had me cut the line and we fished until we limited. I can still see him, fishing away with a fly hooked through his eyelid.

Later on we had the hook removed. He just had that kind of philosophy: Everything in good time, no reason to panic or go crazy. He was as solid as a rock, and he kept me going. I don't know where I'd be if he hadn't been there for me. Working with Hank stabilized me so that I was eventually able to start dealing with my big questions.

Was there a particular turning point that allowed you to start dealing with your questions?

I saw an ad in the paper for a sermon one Sunday, "Discovery in Doubt." The preacher was a guy named Bob Munger who pastored a big church near a university. I knew of him, and I was intrigued by the topic, so I went to church for the first time in three years. I sat right in the back, as far back as I could get. It was very traumatic just being there.

He preached about John in prison, Martin Luther's crisis of faith and his own experiences with doubt. He said that you'll never know faith until you begin to doubt. Suddenly it dawned on me. It was a tremendously freeing experience to think that doubting could actually be something good.

I called him at home and gave him a quick résumé. I said, "I desperately need to talk to you." He started to say no, but he caught the desperation in my voice and said okay.

I wanted answers, but he said he couldn't give me an answer. He asked me if there was anything in the Bible I still believed.

I thought about it and said yes, I believed that the Christian life was morally and ethically sound.

He said, "Forget all the rest and live by that. I suspect that you'll find other elements to grab onto as time goes by."

When I walked out of his office, I felt that I was on the road back. I read *Death Be Not Proud,* in which a reverent agnostic prays to be kept reverent until he can understand more. I read J. B. Phillips's *Your God Is Too Small* and C. S. Lewis's *Mere Christianity.* Those guys helped me to strip all the junk away and find real faith.

If you could go back in time, how would you rearrange things to avoid having a breakdown? Could it have been avoided by a different organizational structure?

Maybe. If I'd had some kind of genuine support system to make me slow down, ask questions, avoid giving pat answers to tough questions, maybe it would have been different. Maybe if I'd examined psychology instead of just relying on God talk, I might have understood what was happening to me. The theory of cognitive dissonance is helpful. When we see that things aren't fitting together like they should, we reduce input and options as a way of protecting ourselves. That was my problem. I knew from the lives around me that things weren't as simple as I wanted them to be, so I just worked harder, ran faster and ignored what I didn't want to see. I paid a terrible price when it all caught up with me.

I do wonder what we are to teach our kids. I know that all the pat answers and systems were a disaster for me. I've tried to plant the seeds of questioning in my kids. I hope that they don't simply become skeptics about everything, but I don't want them to go through what I went through.

Have you talked to pastors who are going through what you went through? Are you able to help others?

I have a friend who's been in the ministry thirty years. We went to school together, and he's the prototypical graduate of our college, which prides itself on its strict, narrow interpretation of Christianity. He criticizes everything to maintain order.

My sense is that he does know what is going on, but he's got a built-in defense mechanism that says everything out there is bad. We can't really talk, because he just gets down on everything. He can't stand liberals. He thinks Billy Graham is evil. The New Age movement—boy, he can go on about that!

Again, it's cognitive dissonance. One response is to close out people who try to help you. I'm not sure that I was a whole lot different, although I wasn't as deeply entrenched, perhaps.

Christ came to set us free, but it's easy to buy into a program and forget about simple faith. Now I have fewer answers, more questions ... and faith.

Part 2

No Blueprints

Keeping Up
with Rapid
Growth

4

He's a tanned, lean, athletic-looking man in his fifties. In my motel room I see one of his television commercials—a short, restrained spot that demonstrates an understanding of the television medium. In the commercial he lets viewers know that his church welcomes seekers, and asks them to visit. The spot is well executed, lacking the schmaltzy histrionics of a televangelist's pitch.

When I arrive for my appointment I'm a bit overwhelmed by the size of the church buildings, which are the biggest I've been in. The parking lot could service a medium-sized airport. Yet it's easy to find the office, and the secretary is friendly and easygoing.

In person he's more intense than he is on television. He's very interested in my book, and after asking me about myself and my reasons for writing the book, he begins to tell me about his congregation's rapid growth and emerging mega-church status.

*　　　*　　　*

I came here in 1970, and the church had been going for about a year. We had sixty-five people back then. Now we have six thousand. We have five regional pastors who marry, bury, counsel and hold meetings. Some of them serve up to eight hundred families. We've started five new churches in other areas.

I came here from another state. We say we "did time" there because none of us liked it much, but all of my children were born there. Everything was smaller and slower. The pace here is much more rapid. We didn't really expect to be in a church this big.

The role of a senior pastor changes when the church grows to this size. About 95 percent of the people don't expect to know you. You really don't know the populace when a church gets this big, but they know who you are. Tuesday I was out soul-winning, and a guy was raking leaves in his yard. I asked him if he knew where this address was, and he said, "Oh, hello, pastor." It happens a lot, especially when I go to the store.

In a way, I don't like it. I was in the hardware store the other day, on my day off. I was wearing shorts, and a guy behind me touched my leg. *He laughs.* The guy was just kidding, but he said, "Hey, I didn't know pastors had hair on their legs!" Everybody knows me, but I don't know them, so in that way it's different from being the pastor of a smaller church where it's mutual. I didn't know who that person was.

It's hard to have private time if we stick around town. A couple of times a year my wife and I just go out of state, where nobody knows us and nobody can get to us.

Quite often somebody here in town will recognize me and want me to solve a problem for them. I understand it, but in a way I resent it. I'm kind of a workaholic, and I rarely get one full day a week off. I take off Friday afternoon, but we have Friday services, and sometimes I don't get out of here until two or three o'clock. I try to take Saturday morning off too. After working a fifty- or sixty-hour week I like to be left alone.

I'm learning to say, with a smile on my face, "I'd like to help you, but today's my day off." Really, most of them understand. I've gotten bolder. I tell them that there are twenty-five other pastors on staff to help them.

A new member said once, "I have no idea what you do. I just thought pastors came down out of heaven on Sunday to preach and then went back up. I don't have a clue what you do during the week."

I was out soul-winning one night, and the guy in the gas station recognized me. "What are you doing?" he asked. I told him I was working. "You work nights?" he said. He was shocked. I told him I usually work about four nights a week.

Even with all the specialists we have here, it's amazing how many calls I take—how many plates I have to keep spinning. I interface with the office staff, the teaching staff, the pastoral staff. I get about twenty calls a week from other pastors around the country, asking my advice on things. I sat down and mapped it out and found that I was involved in forty-five distinct areas of ministry and administration here.

As the church gets bigger, the role changes. My favorite thing is soul-winning, which I used to do about four nights a week. Now it's down to one night a week.

I do no hospital visits, no weddings, almost no funerals. The other pastors do that. That kind of personal ministry is getting replaced by arm's-length ministries. I don't revel in administrating from behind closed doors, but sometimes you have to pull in your horns and get behind the door, or the freight train will run you down.

All the church-growth experts tell us that the megachurch is the church of the nineties. By 1997, 70 percent of all churches will be megachurches, or on their way to becoming megachurches. Right now, about 7 percent are. There are a lot of little churches that will be closed in three or four years because they won't adapt and change.

Sometimes I feel like I'm being drowned. There's no modeling for leading a megachurch, and it can be pretty scary. It's like riding a wild tiger. If you stay on, it's a wild ride and you don't know where you're going. But if you get off, you'll get eaten.

I always knew that we wanted to keep growing, but when we hit three thousand members a couple of years ago I was amazed. Now we have six thousand and we're still growing.

Right now we've outgrown this facility and are looking at a $25 million relocation. If you'd told me back in 1970 that I'd be involved in anything like this, I'd have said, "You're crazy." Back then we thought that three hundred was maxed out for a church.

I'm in my fifties, so I remember the storefront generation. The traffic won't bear it today. The baby-boomer generation won't go to a church like that because it can't offer the programs they want for themselves and their kids.

There's no place to get the expertise, though. You have to invent things as you go along. We're always writing policy.

With a budget of $7 million a year, and eighty employees, we're one of the biggest businesses in this town. We woke up one morning and said, "Hey, we own twenty vehicles—cars, trucks, buses." We have to shuttle people in from off-site because of the parking problem.

We're moving rapidly, and folks who can't handle change can't belong to a church like this. In the book of Acts, it was like one explosion followed by another explosion. The church was always changing and growing, so we shouldn't worry that it's doing the same thing now.

It's projected that this church could hit thirty thousand by the late 1990s. We have one church we started in a town west of here that has eight hundred people after only sixteen weeks. Another one is two years old and has seven hundred.

Part of it is theology. God is still a God of miracles, but he's hampered by our lack of faith. We have to believe in miracles. I have a sign in my office that says that you should only attempt things so miraculous that without God you're lost.

Another change is that churches today need to be "seeker-friendly." That's a buzzword now. It means that your parking lot, your service, your whole operation has to make seekers feel welcome. If it doesn't, you won't have conversions.

People today shy away from the convulsive "hold 'em by the jugular" conversion. Those are still accepted in Latin America, but here people will run if that's the way it's done. Yet you still have to hold to the biblical message of sin and salvation.

This is the age of anonymity. People don't want to be exposed like they did in other times. So many of the new condo complexes have security people now. You can't just go around knocking on doors. If you don't have an appointment, you can't get in. They don't want you there.

There's a danger in growing so fast, and changing so much, that you'll lose the message and just water down. That's why I'm such a radical biblicist. I only preach expositionally—to protect myself from fads. Oh, sometimes I'll preach on a current topic, but people don't want to come and hear some guy's opinion; they want a biblical message. So I just go through the Bible, book by book. I figure that if I do it that way, we'll get to all the passages that need to be heard. I've been preaching that way for about fourteen years.

Nonbelievers have respect for that kind of preaching. I'm not a great preacher, but the Word has the ring of authority. People know when they sit down that they aren't just hearing some guy's opinion.

One nonbeliever even bought a Bible to follow along. He told me that he knew the Bible was an important book and he appreciated the chance to go through it.

We tape television spots, but we're not going to televise our services. People don't want to watch church on television anymore. The people who film our television spots think of it as marketing, but I think of it as penetration. You have to speak to the culture using the language of the media—which is short, concise chunks.

We did one spot in a bar, with all the liquor bottles behind me. I didn't try to condemn the bar scene, but I said that if you were looking for answers you should try Jesus instead. One of the camera guys asked me, "What do you mean, answers? Answers to what?" He said that he went to bars not to get drunk but to meet what he called his "bar buddies." He said it was a chance to spill his guts every now and then. We talked for a while, and eventually I was able to lead him to the Lord.

It's a different kind of ministry than I first entered. My job, and the job of our other pastors, is more to train than to directly minister. We believe it's better to teach someone to be a teacher than to teach, better to train soul-winners than to win souls, better to equip a counselor than to counsel, because that way we are multiplying ourselves.

My job, according to Ephesians 4:11-12, is to equip the saints for ministry, not to do ministry.

At the age of forty I woke up and realized that I was doing too much. By trying to do every aspect of the ministry I was headed for a heart attack. Now the ministry has multiplied.

To people who don't like the changing role of their pastor as the church grows, I'd say that they need to reexamine their beliefs in the light of Scripture, not in the light of tradition.

A fellow who visited here from Chuck Swindoll's church told me that he liked this church better. He said, "I've never shaken his hand like I'm shaking yours." I told him, when you've written forty-five books and taken a hundred phone calls a week and spoken all over the world, you look at things differently. If Chuck Swindoll had to shake your hand, he'd have to shake everybody's hand. You'd be stealing his productivity.

Hanging On
in the Inner
City

5

The brick church building was built at the turn of the century, when this inner-city neighborhood was solidly WASP and middle class. To get to the pastor's office I pass through the Vietnamese Friendship Association's offices, which are decorated with the precommunist flag and photos of a vanished, cosmopolitan Vietnam. A Samoan chief is taking a smoke break on the stairs leading to the pastor's office.

The Samoan Chiefs Association and a multicultural day care, filled with black, white, Lao and Vietnamese kids, share space in the meandering halls and offices of the well-worn church building.

The pastor is a white man in his fifties. He's solidly built, and with his thick chest and thinning crew cut he looks like a military officer. His office is lined with the usual bookshelves, reminding me that I am, after all, in a mainline Protestant church.

* * *

*T*his is a church in transition. It's been in transition for quite a while—first from a white middle-class to a black working-class congregation, and now to Southeast Asian. The blacks are moving farther out, and the Vietnamese, Cambodian and Laotian families are moving in.

Churches like things to be the way they were. They're not good at transition, so it becomes a tremendous teaching and preaching job to help them *want* to make the transition, let alone accomplish it. I preach and teach on this subject every chance I get. The church just celebrated its ninetieth anniversary, so I preached a series of historical sermons about the church, and I'm finishing up with one about the future of the church.

I think of this as a missionary endeavor. We need to know the population of the area and be willing to reach out to people with different names and faces. We need to be missionaries to carry the gospel across cultural barriers. We're just learning, but a lot of our older white members don't really want to carry the gospel across cultural lines. They want the church to be like it always was.

Usually, a church like this just closes its doors and moves to the suburbs. Traditional wisdom says you build your church on the families with kids, because that's how you keep a steady supply of people.

But all of those people have already moved out to the suburbs, so the members tend to be old. They will either retire and move away or die, unless we replace them with new church members. If we don't, we'll lose a voice in the urban area.

It's terribly discouraging and stressful trying to keep people focused on that vision. They feel really threatened by it. What threatens them is the little things, the trivialities, that in the grand scheme of things don't really matter. For instance, the women's group who take care of the kitchen are almost all old-timers. They're middle-aged and older white ladies who have been here since they were children. They were all upset because the Laotian women weren't cleaning up well enough. There were cockroaches in the place. Well! What do they expect of someone from the mountains who has always cooked over a fire in the dirt and drawn water from a stream? Those Laotians had never seen a kitchen until recently. Somebody has to show them. They want to learn! I told the women that they need to show the Laotians exactly what they want them to do. And they can't expect to show them just once.

"What if we put up signs?" they asked.

For crying out loud! These folks, the hill tribe people, don't even have an alphabet for their own language. How are they going to read a sign?

No, we're just learning how to help those folks, let alone effectively evangelize them.

We have two English as a Second Language classes going for elderly Laotians. Some of these people have been here for several years but still can't even say hello in English.

The needs are enormous. We have a lot of Vietnamese coming into the neighborhood who were in the so-called reeducation camps. In other words, they'd been locked up in prison for five to fifteen years. We offered a Saturday ESL class for them, expecting ten to twenty people. Seventy showed up!

I see this as a tremendous opportunity to spread the gospel, but too many of my older church members see it as a threat. It really hurts and wears you down when week after week people are complaining about the little things. "They" don't clean up the kitchen. Who cares? That kind of stuff gets real old.

But look what's happening to the community. In 1980 it was about one-third white, one-third black and one-third Asian. In 1990 it was 38 percent Asian, 36 percent black and 26 percent white. The people who want to live in the community and build homes and businesses are the Vietnamese. The church needs to be here! But teaching that is terribly stressful and frustrating.

There are five or six church members who work with the ESL program. They have gotten to know and appreciate the people. I just hope and pray that we can hold the church together as we incorporate new people into the body. I'd hate to see the church fold before the transition can be completed.

There's an Indian pastor from Singapore, which has always been a multiethnic society. He's working in a church that has simultaneous translation for eleven different languages! Then they worship and pray together. That appeals to me—the incorporation of everybody into the one body. They have midweek fellowships and Bible studies in their own languages, but the body isn't just white or black or Lao or Cambodian. The fellowship is of the believers.

We do have a foundation group in this church of Vietnamese. We got a Vietnamese on our elder board not too long ago, so it's happening. But with all of the younger white people moving away and the older white people resisting change, I don't know if we can hang on.

You have to have a strong group of mature Christians that hangs in for the duration.

Young families leave because the schools are bad, there's too much crime. Maybe that's so, but I've lived here for fourteen years and I feel as comfortable as I do anywhere else in the city. The media tend to portray this area as a pit. I like it here. I like the mix of people, the variety of experiences.

There's a support group of seven pastors from our denomination who are in this area. We meet together once a week to share, pray, laugh and cry. If it wasn't for those guys, I'd go crazy and chuck it.

We went to Chicago for a four-week training session in a ministry there. It used to be a church and a radio ministry in a neighborhood that turned black over the years. The church members moved away. So did the radio ministry. Out to the safe, pleasant suburbs. But—*he laughs*—they couldn't sell the property because their charter said it had to be used for Christian ministry in perpetuity.

Well, they became a church and school for the neighborhood, and that's a thriving ministry. The pastors and most of the teachers are white. Almost the whole church and school are black. They've remained in the neighborhood, and they are discipling people. I talked to one neighborhood fellow who met Christ through those people and is a changed man. He was a hard-core criminal and drug freak. But they discipled him, and when they retire they'll have guys like him to carry on.

We caught the vision there, and we're trying to duplicate it. We're trying to make connections with suburban churches. Some of them are open to helping in a real way. If you're going to run a ministry in the inner city, you need people and money.

The trouble is that I'm overextended just doing my job here. If I go out to the suburbs to get people on board, then my ministry here suffers. As pastors of urban ministries we don't have time to go out to the other churches. That's a whole ministry in itself. You can't just go out once. It's an ongoing thing—making contacts, helping people along—so we hired a woman to do that part of it. She's a great communicator, and she's doing a first-class job.

Urban ministries are the big need in today's society. The cities are falling apart. They are in chaos. And where's the church? Out in the suburbs.

I was never trained to do this job. There are forty distinct cultures in this area. You have to be a missionary to know how to reach them and disciple them for Christ. Seminaries don't even touch on that kind of training. Well, one of ours supposedly does, but it's woefully inadequate.

Our cities are like the Third World. Our denomination has no church in downtown Detroit! Chicago closed fourteen hospitals in the downtown area in the last three years. To minister in that situation you need health ministries, tutoring ministries, nutrition, child care. There's not a major U.S. city that's not in chaos.

But where are all our new churches being built? Out in the suburbs. What about the cities? We may become a big thriving church in the next century, but with no heart! We'll just be a bunch of contented suburban churches running programs for ourselves and building buildings for our own use.

I really disagree with the notion that every church has to be self-supporting. We send missionaries overseas. We don't expect their churches to be self-supporting, because they're "missionaries." What do you call a church in downtown Chicago, where the gangs were having daily firefights between two buildings in the Cabrini Green housing project? It's like Lebanon over there. We went into those buildings. They're like prisons! One massive housing project feeds three elementary schools. Those kids live and go to school and die in that environment. Where's the church? You've really got me on my soapbox now! I'm sorry, but I get really hot about this.

Urban ministry is a "slug-it-out" deal. It's not glamorous. You don't get big results. You work hard and see very little return by worldly standards.

It's a hard, frustrating struggle. And it's death to your career. You can kiss your career goodby if you choose to work here. People in the denomination figure that a guy who works away year after year in a poor church with a hundred members must be a loser.

One of our churches over in the suburbs is going ahead with a $7.5 million building project! For what? They already have a nice building. Think about what you could do down here with that money. Think of the lives that could be changed!

We visited a downtown church in Chicago. Great big beautiful downtown church, with stained-glass windows and a fabulous organ. It was like a cathedral! And there were 150 people there on a Sunday. They're putting all that energy into keeping a building going!

Everybody is interested in the megachurch. Something for everyone!

I meet all these bright guys from seminary, and where do they all end up after they graduate? Not down here!

There's a guy in one of the megachurches who started an inner-city school for dropouts and druggies. What a great idea! But he gets a lot of flak about it. People think it's a waste of time and money because the numbers are so small. One guy finding Christ, getting off drugs and earning a high-school diploma isn't enough "success" to justify the expense.

I went to a retirement party for one of our preachers recently, and he told us about a dream he had. He said, "I dreamed I went with God across the Red Sea to a beautiful land full of beautiful people and lovely buildings—a dream land. But God said, 'This is not the Promised Land.' Then we went farther into the desert, until we came to a place full of AIDS and poverty and sickness, and God said, 'That's the Promised Land.' " Then he said, "There are preachers who are real gems working in these ministries." Everybody clapped. That surprised me, because I always get the feeling that they think I'm crazy. Nobody really has any respect for us.

The inner-city pastors I meet with are all in their upper fifties or early sixties like me. I don't know what will happen when we all retire in the next few years. I'm afraid that they won't find anyone to fill those slots, and the churches might just close down.

If the church is going to stay in the inner city, the church will have to take the inner city seriously and commit time, money and people on a long-term basis. Pastors won't come here if they can't make a living—especially pastors with young families.

You'll also have to train pastors to work here. Seminary will have to be a radically different experience than it is now. All that stuff about predestination and election is good, but it doesn't help you to minister here. I'd make the seminarians immerse themselves in an urban ministry for two or three years, and then do the theology.

Come to think of it, I'd make the professors work in the inner city too. You can't minister to people until you really understand and know them. The seminaries are set up to train people to go into the suburbs, or to teach in seminaries. The professors write obscure books that nobody reads, and they talk to each other. You can't teach what you don't know. It all focuses on the suburban lifestyle.

There's an urban ministry in Chicago that started by tutoring four students. Now it's tutoring hundreds of people. It's making a huge change in people's lives. Giving them hope. Big corporations like AT&T are now involved. They send their people to teach, because the businesses in Chicago can't find people with the basic skills to work for them.

Imagine having no hope and being helped in such a tangible way by the church. Those people are having their lives changed by the church. That's how you earn the right to share the gospel.

This city is not as bad a place as Chicago or Detroit, but I can see the seeds. We have everything we need to fall into complete chaos and despair. The churches are packing up and leaving with the white middle class. But some of us want the church to stay and be a voice, to bring the gospel to everyone. I know that the suburbs have problems like everybody else. But they have more options. More access. There are lots of counselors in the suburbs. The people over there have access to good educations; they speak English; they have more money. Much of what they need is convenience. People here have life-or-death needs. They haven't heard the gospel.

Baby Boomers and the Talking Bush

6

He's a veteran of the sixties who has held to the orthodox faith, but not the peripheral traditionalism of his denomination. His church, in a growing bedroom community, is geared toward the needs of young families—people of his own generation whom he feels the church has shut out.

We meet in his home on a rainy afternoon and share a soft drink. He's a humorous, engaging man, quick to make a joke, but also very serious. As we begin the interview, I discover how deeply he grieves for the people of his generation who have left the church.

*　　　*　　　*

I pastored a metropolitan church in the Great Lakes area. It was in a city neighborhood that was low-income. The church had been in a twenty-four-year membership decline. It's what they call *ethnicitis,* when the congregation no longer reflects the ethnic or socioeconomic makeup of the neighborhood. The members move out to the suburbs and come in for church.

Of the baby-boom generation, 20 percent of those baptized in our denomination are still there. In other words, we've lost 80 percent of the boomers.

The church I was pastoring is much like a lot of our churches—

and other churches, for that matter. It's based on the assumptions of the fifties. It meets the needs and preferences of the fifties generation. That's what finally led to my leaving. I couldn't handle the stress of trying to be a bridge for the two generations when the older generation wouldn't give up power.

I was hired to be a bridge, because the church knew that it would cease to exist in twenty years unless it changed and began to draw in younger people and the people in the neighborhood. What they didn't realize was the cost of changing.

We began to reach out to families that had moved into the neighborhood for exactly the reasons the church members had moved out. The young social workers, teachers and artists liked the old, affordable houses and the racial mix of the neighborhoods. They saw all this as attractive—the acceptance, for instance, of biracial marriages.

I was the change agent, and frankly, my values lay with the people in the neighborhood. I have a pastor's heart, and I wanted to be there for the older parishioners, but I saw things more the way those funky younger families saw things.

Church people are supposed to be nice, so they tend to act out problems and conflicts behind the scenes. We fought a lot of battles, and some of those battles left scars.

One example of a "battle" revolved around the Communion table. It seems really trivial, but it serves as an example.

I should preface this story with a little anecdote. When we were doing some repairs after a tornado ripped the roof off the sanctuary and did some other damage, we moved the building's entrance. The old entrance had required latecomers to enter at the front of the building, so we put a new one near the back. That made it easier to conduct a service.

Well, one of the influential women required that the deacons unlock the old door just for her so that she could enter the church the way she always had. These folks found tradition pretty important.

Anyway, the pulpit was rather large, with a big rail in front and two chairs behind, so that the pulpit area was pretty crowded. It was also a pretty formidable barrier between me and the people of the congregation when I tried to preach.

To make it worse, there was a second barrier in front. The Communion table was always decorated with a large floral display that was sometimes so tall I had to almost peer through the foliage to see the congregation. Then there was a large bronze cross that also decorated the altar. On weeks when the flowers were so tall that they blocked the cross, the cross was put on top of a stack of hymnals. I felt like a talking bush.

Three times in seven years I formally requested that we put a simple chalice or the open Scriptures on the table instead of the flowers. I asked if we could just move the table. I consulted a professor of speech and communication, who told us that the setup was a real block to any kind of communication.

Well, if the preaching of the gospel is really one of the most important parts of my job, you'd think we'd break down the barriers. But the table, cross and flowers had to stay.

One lady told me, "You're changing my church. The church I was baptized and married in. The church where I buried my loved ones."

The thing is, it was true. I did want to change some things that I saw as obstacles. And to reach the people in the neighborhood, especially the younger people, I would have had to do things that would alienate the old folks who'd been in that church all their lives.

One of the few sneaky things I did was a few months after the battle of the table settled down: when the table was moved for a wedding, I actually hid the cross in the basement. Some of the people panicked, but that's how desperate I was.

You know, pastors are supposed to have all this power and authority, but I couldn't even move the furniture around. Imagine a CEO who couldn't move his own desk. Especially when it could be demonstrated rationally, and on the basis of fact, that moving it would increase his effectiveness.

I didn't lie, but I never volunteered information about the cross—that is, until one of the deacons proposed a pledge drive to get a new one. The thing was going to cost eight or nine hundred bucks to replace, so it suddenly turned up.

Tradition is good, but traditionalism, the need to follow tradition for its own sake, is a problem.

When I took that job, I bought a home a block from the church and people told me I was nuts. The church lawyer, who helped negotiate the deal, told me I was foolish to make an investment in that neighborhood. I guess that should have told me something at the outset.

I made friends in the neighborhood, and a core group of those new friends came into the church. But I struggled in many cases inviting some of my new friends to the church and having them put up with all the garbage. I just hated to dump all that on them.

We ended up leading a lot of our inner-city neighbors to Christ and having them move into other churches. They heard and accepted the gospel, but they couldn't fit into our congregation. I was struck with the situation when I heard a fellow from the Vineyard church ask the question "If you weren't paid to, would you attend this church?" My answer was no. I believe in serving where you're called, and I know that sometimes that means being in a place that you wouldn't necessarily choose, but after eight years in that church I realized that I wouldn't want to worship there, and I didn't want my kids to grow up with that as their church experience.

I felt a lot of stress over the generation and traditionalism obstacles. People who came to the church, if they were at all different, felt a sense of unwelcoming and judgment. The church is supposed to be loving yet firm, but often we get it upside-down.

I really got worn down doing maintenance and attending to the squeaky wheels. I don't have the gift of mercy. In the Midwest they have a very traditional sense of who the pastor is. He's the one who prays at the potluck and gets put up on a pedestal as the community chaplain. He's expected to do all the hospital visits and visit in the home of each member at least once a year. My gifts are in the area of teaching and spiritual leadership, yet most of my time was spent in areas that aren't my strength.

My dad was a pastor. He's a workaholic, a classic Type A personality. He gave everything to his church, and as kids we felt shortchanged. I think that he created a dependency, so that he ended up enabling dysfunctional churches that couldn't operate without him. When you end up playing all the roles, the spiritual direction is short-changed.

In Acts, when they first set up the elders, it was to free Paul and the apostles from the daily tasks so that they could teach and preach and disciple. But if you say this publicly, people think you're somehow shirking your job. I've even heard it said that a pastor is a sort of prostitute: "You're paid to give us love."

When you put the pastor up on a pedestal, you can't criticize him to his face. The blanket assumption in the church seems to be that it's okay to go behind his back. I ended up feeling like I was shadow-boxing. There were only three or four people who would come to me and address issues straightforwardly.

I went to a seminar on church healing. It was great, and I wanted to have a seminar at the church. But as the deadline approached, two-thirds of the church leaders dropped out. They felt they couldn't take the risk.

Why all the fear? Many pastors don't listen. We have a lot of ego, and there are plenty of horror stories about pastors nailing people to the wall. I watched my father do this. He'd turn key people against "troublemakers," keep people out of areas of leadership. He felt that you were either for him or against him.

Elderly people, who expect you to visit them when they get sick and to eventually bury them, don't want to alienate you. They have a need to like and approve of the pastor, and to be liked and approved of. This makes it hard for them to criticize you to your face.

You listen to the stories about your predecessors, and you see what the fears are. I wonder *(he laughs)* what stories they're telling about me now.

On paper, a hierarchical denomination like ours should be one of the best ways of governing church bodies. You have supervision from the larger body, and your congregation can't just fire you like the Baptists can. But the session is really a permission-withholding body. You're given responsibility, but not authority. You can't even move the Communion table when it's blocking the pulpit.

Sin,
Not Skin

7

He's a huge bear of a man—a former pro football player with a chest like a refrigerator and a neck like a fireplug. One of three senior pastors in a large, suburban church, he's unusual in that he's a black pastor in a mostly white, suburban congregation. It's an upscale community, full of young professional families.

His study is in a professional office building, part of a suite of rooms that make up the church offices. Services are held elsewhere. The walls are lined with the usual bookshelves, but there are also pictures of horses and big game—hunting and fishing pictures showing huge trophies. He's dressed casually, in a college sweatshirt and baggy cotton pants.

I ask him about the switch from big league football, with its accompanying fame, prestige and money, to the role of pastor.

*   *   *

I played football to get an education. I never intended to make it a career. I had always wanted to go to Dallas Theological Seminary to prepare for the ministry, and when the Dallas Cowboys drafted me I figured I could take classes during the off season. That didn't work out, though, because I had to go back to Louisiana for family reasons.

Football was fine, though, so I stayed on. But after three seasons I'd hurt my knee pretty bad. I could have played longer, but I wanted to be able to walk when I got older, so it seemed like the time to move on.

I started out as a youth pastor in a big church in a mostly white suburb. Sometimes people would ask me why I went into youth min-istry after all the money and fame of playing pro football. I'd tell them I was in it for the money. *He laughs.* I don't say that now, because it's not a very funny joke, with all the televangelist scandals and all. Now people would probably just nod and say, "Um-humm!"

I always had a strong desire to work with kids, and I saw the youth ministry as a step up from pro ball. I had made a commitment that I would work to be a role model for kids, because I really hadn't had any Christian male role models in my life. That's probably why I got in so much trouble as a kid.

My mom never married, you see. My uncle taught me to be tough. He said to never trust whites. He said you gotta be three times as good as a white man to succeed the same as him. There's some truth to that, but you can't let the negative get you down. You have to follow the Lord and look forward.

I'm copastor with three people here. We have about fifteen hundred people in our church. We wanted it to be a truly interracial worship service, and we have about one-quarter blacks and other minorities now. That's pretty good for this part of town.

When I became a senior pastor we lost some folks, but the Lord replaced them. We lost more when I married a white woman. Black people told me, "If you marry a white woman you can forget about ever ministering to African-American people again!"

I feel bad about those folks, but in the Lord's eyes it's sin not skin that matters.

*   *   *

What I like most about being a pastor is that there's no limit to what I can do, where I can go, whom I can touch. Like most people, I love the idea of doing something I enjoy and still getting paid for it. That's every man's dream.

On the other hand, it's an awesome responsibility to say, "Thus saith the Lord." That's not something I can take lightly.

Have you ever said, "Thus saith the Lord," and later realized that he didn't say that?

No. I spend a lot of time in the Word. There's times when I read what the Lord says and I wish he hadn't said it. It's hard to preach the hard gospel to people if they just say, "Well, I know the Lord said it, but I don't care." But I won't say "God says" unless it's written right there in the Word. If it's there, I preach it. Whether people like it or it's out of fashion or whatever.

Divorce and remarriage, for example. The Word is pretty clear about that. We live in a time of easy divorce, where you can just decide to back out of the commitment you made before God. People want easy forgiveness so they can just do what they want. The church has to stand for repentance and restoration, not just easy forgiveness.

That's difficult for the people going through it. They don't like to be told that they have sinned. We try to practice Christian discipleship in our church. We talk to the person one on one, then with one or two others. Sometimes we have to bring someone before the church, but that's pretty rare because if you follow the biblical steps you usually don't get to that point.

I'm trying to teach the kids about Christian discipline so that when they get older they'll expect it. We have too many Christians who just want easy acceptance.

Psychology and psychiatry have been more detrimental than helpful. Some things are just caused by sin. This idea of "you're OK, I'm OK" gets us off the track. Where in the Word does God say we should seek a good self-image? All this high self-esteem is not a biblical norm. All this talk about codependency and dysfunctional families can get us away from admitting to sin and doing something about it.

The Bible says that husbands must love their wives like their own bodies, but that's not what people want to hear. They want to be able to cast their wives or husbands away.

Do you find that people question your knowledge or authority on questions of marriage and family because you're young? How does a wealthy, successful man in his fifties respond when you give advice about life?

Sometimes people think that because my own kids are young, I don't understand what they're going through. I've only been married a few years and I'm happy, so what do I know about their unhappiness? But I know what the Word says. That's what's important. I tell them, "I'll hold you accountable to the Word, and maybe you can do the same for me when I get in trouble."

You are one of the very few churches around that's truly integrated. Is this by accident, or do you have an agenda?

The institutional church often misses trends. Right now, most church people associate by hair. *He laughs heartily.* That's right! By how straight or kinky our hair is. We have churches that are all white or all black or all Asian or Hispanic. We've gone that way for years. But the trend in society is more toward intermarriage. As more and more people intermarry, there'll be a big group of folks who don't fit easily into an all-white or an all-black or whatever church. I can understand that because my wife is white.

Once you marry out of your race, you just don't fit into a racially pure church. Especially if that racial purity is a deliberate thing, because the racially pure church is trying to keep people from mixing with them.

This whole race question is going to continue to hold us back. Look in the Bible at Boaz and Naomi and Ruth. Or David, who was descended from Rahab. God didn't command everyone to stick purely to their own kind. But we do. Black churches are worse than white churches sometimes. We keep trying for purity when no one else is. In business we don't try to keep racially pure. Not in sports, or even the army. Why? Because it's wrong. It holds people back, and it holds whole organizations back from being what they could be.

A lot of it just comes down to likes and dislikes. We like a certain style of music, or preaching, or fellowship, because that's all we've ever known. Then we say, "This is God's way," when really it's just a matter of our own likes and dislikes.

The church doesn't do enough to teach us how to talk to a brother when he's different from us. If we don't figure it out, we'll be a dying breed. God is interested in sin, not skin. We need to learn how to discern the spirits, to call good good and bad bad.

While churches try to keep themselves "pure," they are living impure lives. I was reading that in one denomination in a city back East, one out of eight churchgoers is having an extramarital affair. Where are the Pauls busting them? Too busy trying to please everyone and make everyone feel good about themselves. Our love is concerned with comfort. God's love is about molding.

I spend a lot of time thinking and praying and preaching about this. Growing up black, without a father, I got in a lot of trouble. Christians should learn and model a healing, put-together life. If we don't, things will just fall apart around us. If we're divided up by our hair and can't keep our promises to our wives and husbands, we're not going to be of much use in this world.

3307

Pastoring a Mexican Church

8

*He's thirty and looks like the stereotypical Southern California surf bum—
blond hair, lanky, tanned body in loose cotton T-shirt and jeans. His speech has
that easygoing surfer modality that gets parodied on "Saturday Night Live."
Nobody would ever peg him as a seasoned missionary who's battled jungle
illness in Brazil. Nor would they guess that he's the pastor of a Mexican church.*

*He splits his time between Tijuana and San Diego. His modest office in the
American church looks across the freeway at a yacht basin and a beach resort.
The Mexican church is perched atop a rocky hill in an area without lights,
sewers or water. The roads are so pitted with holes and ruts that many passenger
cars can't make the trip.*

* * *

I grew up in church and accepted the Lord at an early age. When
I was sixteen, a youth pastor laid a heavy challenge on me to give
my whole life to the Lord and not hold anything back.

I was real gung-ho, and when I was seventeen I went to South
America with him. Everybody else discouraged me from going. They
said it was okay to want to be a missionary or pastor, but I shouldn't
get off the track. You know, high school, college, seminary. Get a
toolbox full of tools and then go into the ministry. But it seemed right
to just go, like Paul did.

That's probably not right for everybody, but I just felt a very strong

The Library of
Chuck Sackett

call to get on with it. We're not called to be logical, we're called to be obedient.

Well, I got sick for a whole year after that. I was so sick I could hardly do anything. The doctors couldn't figure it out, and everybody said that it was proof that I was jumping the gun. I was really down, because I'd always been a healthy, strong guy and that illness really laid me low. I finally went to a tropical disease center in Panama, but they couldn't do anything for me either.

The next year I went back to the Amazon to work with an un-reached tribe in the jungle. I was bitter at God, because my illness seemed to contradict his leading me to the mission field, but I decided to just sign over the pink slip to my car, cash out and go start the training. The guy I went with takes four guys a year to disciple, and I really felt that I was supposed to go—sick or not.

The training was not just books and study, but sharing life. We had to get ready physically and mentally for the rigors of working in Third World countries. We spent several months in Mexico with the poor and then did a week of desert boot camp. It was about 105 degrees, and we ran and ran. He made it hard, so that we could see each other's worst side. Then we did a week of jungle training camp. After that we were ready to work. We worked with people in the Amazon who haven't heard the Word.

When I came back, I got involved in this church in Tijuana. It was like going to Africa or something. People living in boxes, under pieces of cardboard or plastic. You really see the underside of the Mexican government. All those people just left to fend for themselves. They can only focus on immediate needs, because they never know if they'll be alive the next day.

The U.S. floods the border regions with missionaries. Frankly, some of it seems like a scam. They take pictures of really poor people and then get big donations. Sometimes they just make the Mexican people dependent on them.

I was involved in helping people build their own houses. They *call* them houses. Each one is about 8 by 12. Not even as big as a carport, but it's sure better than a cardboard box. I didn't try to push Bible study. I waited until the people asked.

People came to know the Lord, and I helped them build a church building. We built it together because they wanted to do it. They have a drug rehabilitation center there now.

We also built a public school. Yeah! A public school! Again, it was a felt need. The government mandated a school and sent out a couple of teachers, but there was no building and no books. The kids just came and sat on the rocks. There wasn't even a blackboard. So we built a school and gave it to the government.

Some people in the U.S. really thought that was a waste. Why a public school? They wanted to see converts for their money. But you know, most Christians in the States send their kids to public schools. They wouldn't dream of not sending them.

These people have so little. If they can't get a basic—and I mean basic—education, they'll just be overwhelmed by their problems.

It's really sad. The father leaves the mother, that's a really big problem here, so the mother feels she needs another man. The kids are on the street sniffing glue and paint, and the whole family goes downhill almost overnight. The kids get into gangs and try to get by by stealing.

This is one of the roughest neighborhoods in Tijuana. There are a lot of stabbings here, and it's the largest drug area in the city. Car theft is big here too. A couple of days ago some of the kids were at the dump and saw a nice new car there. Yeah! It was a Mazda. They thought, "Oh boy! Let's strip it! Stereo, seats, wheels, tires . . ." But when they got closer they saw a body behind the wheel. Murder victim. Somebody had wasted him and pushed him and his car into the dump.

The kids stayed away, because it was most likely a drug murder. The police here just round up whoever is around, so the kids split. That's not the first murder victim many of them have seen. Not much of a way to live, huh?

That's why I keep working with the church. Somehow you have to disciple kids so that they see that there's more than scavenging and scamming and dealing dope.

We have classes four or five days a week. Sometimes we do correspondence courses. We have a 6:00 a.m. Bible study. There's about a 90 percent dropout rate, though. We have a core group of about thirty who come regardless of weather, violence or political trouble—which can get pretty hot, by the way. The church service runs at about 80 to 140, depending on how things are going. Most people have to walk to get to church, and as you've seen, there's no sidewalks, no lights and no law up in the barrio.

*   *   *

I never thought about being a pastor. I still don't really. I was helping out, and after a while the people started calling me pastor. I wish that we could find a Mexican pastor, but so far nobody has come. I'm single, and I get help from my church in the States. If a married pastor came to the barrio, he'd probably starve.

Also, Mexican pastors are pretty different. They tend to be pretty secretive, and there's a lot of this "inner circle" mentality. The Mexican pastor is a guy in a dark suit and shiny shoes who expects, and gets, a lot of respect—at least if he has some education. That's okay in the suburbs, I guess, among the wealthier people. But these people in our church are poor, and they don't seem to want, or need, somebody to lord it over them.

Most of them work at hard manual labor six days a week. They barely have enough to survive. They work in factories, assembly plants or construction. A salary of forty to sixty dollars a week is considered great wages for a sixty-hour week. It's like back at the turn of the century in the States. Except that those guys in the factories and mills of Chicago could see things getting better. There was lots of room in the States then. Lots of food. Lots of improvement. Here things just get more crowded and poorer. Now there's talk of a resurgence of cholera.

The biggest problem, when you're trying to disciple these people, is convincing them that there is a tomorrow, let alone an eternity. Life is just such a grind.

When you get a teenager who has no education, no prospects and no father, you've got a pretty alienated and defeated person. Why not just blow your brains out? Why not just sniff some glue or paint and then rob somebody?

Sometimes when I'm back in San Diego, I look out the window at all the wealth and promise. There's free education for anybody who wants it, good doctors, Medicare. We have lots of food. Then I look a little farther down the road and there it is: Mexico. The problems are just overwhelming.

You take all of this quite seriously. What makes you happy?

I don't know if anything makes me happy. That's a good question. I'm not unhappy, but I don't think about being happy. If I am happy, I guess it doesn't happen enough. I feel a satisfaction. No . . . When I see a guy like Carlos, whose life has been such a wreck—drugs, abandonment, crime, prison—walking with the Lord, it's right. It's a privilege to serve, and that makes me feel that what I'm doing is right. But it doesn't make me happy, I guess.

I never wanted to be a pastor. If I could just decide what to do, I'd be back in the Amazon with the unreached tribes. Being a pastor is pretty defeating at times, especially for a young, unmarried guy. You are called upon to counsel people about their marriages and children when you don't really have the expertise or experience in those areas.

I don't think of myself as particularly gifted in the area of church discipline. A gifted leader who was active in our church got a teenager pregnant. He was older, in his thirties. When I talked to him with the deacons, he got downright vicious. Later he married her and wanted to be restored, but he didn't want to admit that he'd done anything wrong.

They really need Mexican leaders. People who know the language and customs better than I do. I'm kind of exotic to them. I seem highly educated and rich. Kind of charmed. They need to see Mexicans— middle-class Mexicans who have made it in their own society—in places of leadership. But the Mexican middle class is not interested in the barrios. I think it embarrasses them.

There was a doctor in Tijuana who taught Bible classes at his house for several months. He had a nice home, like one an American professional would live in. He invited our people over. But when they came, his wife put sheets over all the furniture! It was pretty awkward.

Ministering to poor people when you have access to a rich lifestyle is pretty disorienting. You work a few days with people who struggle to get clean drinking water, then drive half an hour and argue with the American deacons about fixing the air conditioner. I almost had a nervous breakdown a few years ago. I felt like a rubber band being stretched back and forth. I was playing rich man, poor man. Our church in the States is in debt over an organ. I just couldn't care less.

I've learned to keep quiet about my double life, though. People don't want to hear that they're rich. That just makes them defensive.

How did you avoid having the breakdown?

It finally comes down to understanding that you're not working with the whole world. We go to heaven or hell one person at a time. I can only work with the people I'm with, one at a time. I don't want to be callous or cynical, but I've had to become hardened.

You've seen the way people drive. People get run over by cars all the time down here. There's usually no ambulance for them. We have people sitting in church, scratching away at terrible infections. People whose teeth are literally rotten. Is it my job to pull the teeth? You can't do everything.

I don't work with the whole nation. Nobody does. I have to give my best effort and share the Lord's tears. The Bible says that God wants everyone to be saved. Sometimes I look around and wonder how that can be, but I don't believe that God has changed his mind.

The church in the States will never be mobilized for missions. We could take all of our talent and wealth and really do something, but we're too product- and success-oriented.

I saw a flashy, full-page ad in an American paper asking people to give money to a giant clinic here in Mexico. American Christians like that: Big! Successful! Happening! Poverty sells, because people like to give for their own needs. We often use helping the poor as a way to make ourselves feel better—sometimes at the expense of the poor we're supposed to be helping.

We had some American Christians who gathered toys for Christmas. Great! We asked them to let us take them and hide them, so that the kids' own parents could give them a present on Christmas morning. Oh, no! They wanted their youth group to have the experience of giving the presents to the kids. Think about it. When poor kids get presents from rich kids, what have they learned? But if a dad gives a present to his own kid, there's a real bond that's built.

When I ask for support from American Christians, they want to know how many have been saved. They want their own people to get some kind of blessing. I can understand that. The youth pastor wants to have his kids build a house so that they'll experience the act of giving. But a while ago we had a family who needed a house built. It was all set for a youth group who'd raised the 250 dollars for materials to come down and build it. But then the family's child got sick and needed an operation for 250 dollars. I asked if we could use the house money for the operation. No! So they get a house, but their kid dies. Oh, well. The youth group goes home having ministered to the needy.

If I didn't know better, I'd say this was the cynicism you talked about earlier.

Yeah. *He laughs and shakes his head.* Well, you have to build up the national people. You're working with people who have been so beaten down that all they can see is day-to-day survival.

To sum it all up, how do you do that on a concrete, day-to-day level?

Well, tomorrow I'm getting together with Mexican churchmen to dig a pit for an outhouse. We'll talk, and pray, and maybe eat together.

Part 3

If Bigger
Is Better . . .

Living
in the Shadow
of the Big
Churches

9

He's a soft-spoken, genuinely warm fellow who pastored in the Midwest before moving to the Sun Belt. He's in his mid-forties, with kids due to leave the nest in a few years.

When he entered the ministry, he planned to devote his life to pastoring small, conservative churches like those he'd known as a youth. But in this age of church growth and megachurches, he's finding that his aging congregation is just holding its own.

As we talk, he's reflective and thoughtful, but not morose or complaining. He strikes me as a man who is praying his way through a potential turning point in his ministry.

*   *   *

*P*eople read all these books by Swindoll and the others and get all excited. "Did you hear him on the radio?" I feel like I have to keep up. I've only been in two churches in my twenty-eight years of ministry, and they've both been smaller churches. I wonder, "Why can't we get more people?"

I wonder if some guys are just destined to be in churches where huge numbers come in week after week, and others are supposed to labor away with 150. I wrestle with that a lot.

I know a pastor whose wife committed suicide a few years ago. He was in a support group to deal with his grief, and he met a woman whose husband had killed himself. Her husband had been the pastor of a church with a hundred or so members, and he'd go to denominational meetings where they'd ask, "How many did you have this Sunday? How many were saved? How many were baptized?"

She said she'd asked her husband one time, "Why do you go to those meetings? You just come back all depressed and defeated. They don't inspire you. They tear you down." She felt that those meetings contributed to his suicide.

I went to a seminar by a guy who has seven or eight thousand in his church. One of the pastors stood up and asked him, "How do you call on people?"

"I don't call."

"How many funerals do you do?"

"I don't."

"How many marriages, baptisms—"

He said, almost impatiently, "I study and preach. That's what I do. I study eight hours a day and preach the Word."

I just couldn't understand how this worked. It just sounded too cut and dried, so I asked him, "How do you get things going?"

He said, "I don't. I pray and ask God to motivate other people to get things going. I don't start anything. I just preach."

I don't know how he can do it. I wanted to ask him, but I didn't get the time.

People visit big churches and they can get lost if they want to. If they visit my little congregation two or three times, we smell fresh blood! We hound them! If someone goes here a few times and then misses a Sunday, we call them up. I've told my people that maybe we should back off a bit. Maybe we scare people off by overwhelming them before they can try the place out.

In my first church there were a lot of young people, so it wasn't so hard to get things going. Here there are a lot of retired people. The Sun Belt draws a lot of older people, and they're pretty resistant to change. In a small church if you have ten people who resist change, you can't just roll over them like you can in a big church. At least I imagine you could. I think that in a bigger church, people who didn't like the direction you were going would be more likely to just move on.

As we get older, we get more comfortable in our ways. We get scared of change. The biggest problem with an older congregation is that they fear compromising the faith. They get confused between methods and doctrine. You have to change your methods as time goes on, and that makes them worry that you're selling out. They want the church to grow, but they want it to be just like it was when they were young.

What do you do about that? Sometimes you lie awake in bed and think, "Well, there are geriatric doctors who specialize in treating older people. There's a whole service sector set up to meet the needs of older people. Why not a church for senior saints? Why not a specialized church where you could just pack 'em in?" Don't think I haven't considered it.

I also think about moving on, but I don't know where I'd go. I started thinking about leaving my last church after having ten or eleven great years during which I never considered leaving. Then there was an unsettled feeling, and I thought about moving. I started looking around and sending out résumés. I asked pastor friends if they'd heard of anything.

I wasn't running from anything. Partly I got weary of the Midwestern winters and wanted to come out West where I'm originally from. Partly it was that my mother was sick. I just gradually felt the need to move.

I didn't tell anyone in the church. I did confide in one or two close friends, but mostly I just looked quietly. You just slip out résumés, and when they ask for references you give them the names of one or two people, or you give them names from somewhere else.

I waited until I got the new position, and then I announced from the pulpit that I would be leaving in one month. They were shocked. I'm not sure that was the right thing to do.

Maybe you should tell people that you're thinking about moving on. That you've been there maybe a bit too long. I wonder if the congregation should be part of the process of looking for a new position, but that's pretty scary. They might lose confidence and wonder if you're just marking time. Then if nothing comes up for you but they've found someone new, that could be another problem.

In the circles I've run in, pastors just slip out résumés and keep it quiet. Then they move.

Why
Should God
Give Us
Converts?

10

We meet in the parsonage. He has warned me that his kids are sick with the flu, but I come anyway. The parsonage is on the same lot as the church. Both buildings are plain, but well kept up. His wife offers me a Coke, and I sit on the floor with him as he patches a playpen mattress with tape. He's meticulous and thrifty in his use of the tape. Many people would have thrown the mattress out and bought a new one, but he sees an opportunity to save a few bucks and he's a good steward.

He's friendly, but wary. He asks me about myself, where I go to church and so forth, before he opens up. We talk around doctrine, church membership and where we went to school.

As we chat, the phone rings. His wife brings it to him, and he talks to a woman who needs food. He tells her to come by in an hour and he'll see what he can do.

Sipping our Cokes, we begin to discuss his role as a pastor in this small island community.

*   *   *

*T*he church has been here about thirty years. We have about thirty-three members, and we haven't grown in quite a while. The average age is thirty-eight to forty-eight, with a lot of people in their fifties. It's an older group than I'd like to see.

We don't have any people in their twenties. There are no young families with babies. We did have a couple about a year ago, but when she got pregnant they left. A lot of young couples leave when they start having kids. It's not as much trouble to get money and food on the mainland as it is on this island. When you're young and childless you don't mind living in a little trailer, heating with wood and working at odd jobs. You can fish, cut wood, etc. But it's really tough for a young family to make it out here.

The woman who just called me is a good example. She's a single mom and lives in a trailer, and she had her power cut off recently. She doesn't really have any marketable job skills. I wonder why she doesn't go to the mainland and get a job. There are lots of entry-level jobs—waitressing even—on the mainland. Here there's very little, even in the summer. In the winter it really dries up. But it is a beautiful place, one of the most beautiful I've seen. I guess it's hard to leave.

I'm not from around here. I come from the South, so I'm not as attached to the location as some of the members are.

* * *

When I think about the focus of my ministry here, I have to say that I'm a bit of a flounderer. I've been doing a lot of reading and praying, and it seems to me that the main role of the church, and therefore my role, is to make disciples. That's what Jesus did. I've really struggled to make that work, but it just doesn't go. I've set up small groups, but a high percentage of my people have had some Bible school training, and they're not teachable. People in this community are known for their individualism and self-reliance. They don't defer to the pastor or assume he knows more about the Word than they do.

They seem to feel they know more than me, but they aren't really doing anything with their knowledge.

I'm waiting for God to provide some people who can be a vehicle for a discipling ministry.

When I try to lead in that direction I get resistance. There's one man in the congregation from whom I might get some response. He's the one spark of hope.

I'm trying to determine the precise method, to find out how God wants me to proceed, and then really begin this fall, but I'm not too hopeful. There's a pattern here that emerges. There's lots of study, but no action. You can't just sit around studying the Word without acting on what you read, but that's kind of the pattern here.

People are doing the steps all right, but without a vision. I ask them, "If someone wanted to become a Christian, what would you do?" Most of them don't really know. I want to start some small studies with books that will help them to have at least a minimal understanding of how to disciple a new believer.

These people want to see souls saved and people discipled, but it's almost as if they just expect people to walk in the door, and then I will win them to Christ and disciple them. I asked them, "Why should God give us converts? We don't deserve converts."

We did have a "get started" program that was very good. I had hoped that it would give us a focus for our outreach. We started going through it on a weekly basis, but only one man went all the way through. Everyone else dropped out.

Finding a focus is the first step to a living, witnessing church. But we face a spiritual enemy, and he'll help us to do anything that will derail us from our real task. I think the enemy will *help* us with programs and get-togethers as long as we're kept from doing what we're supposed to be doing. I feel it: a strong attack from the enemy.

But you can't just blame it all on the devil. It's our sinful nature that makes us resist doing God's work. God has given us the power to resist. But we can be on the cutting edge of our Christian walk if we trust in him.

Most of us, and I do mean *us,* are not that sharp spiritually. We go in cycles. Sometimes we run the race at a sprint, sometimes we just sit and rest. I'm not sure what the main obstacles are. I wouldn't rule out myself as the major obstacle in this church.

Anything is possible by the power of God, but when you don't know what the obstacle is, you don't know what to pray for. With the church being so small, and the only one of our denomination on the island, I don't really have many people to talk to about these things. I'm a bit isolated.

As far as close friends and confidants go, I go to my wife. There aren't other pastors here on the island that I can go to. There are a dozen or so churches of our denomination in this area of the state, and the pastors have a monthly prayer time. I have one good friend who's a pastor in the city, and I used to see him there. But it costs twenty dollars for gas and ferry, so I can't afford to go every month. It used to be a brown-bag lunch, but then the other pastors changed it to a breakfast in a restaurant, which raised the cost even more, so I don't go anymore.

My friend did drive up a while ago, though. I walked on the ferry, which is a lot cheaper than taking a car, and he picked me up at the dock. We had a good time of prayer and fellowship. I'm hoping we can do that some more. He's a good one for me. He tells it to me straight.

*　　*　　*

When you are the pastor in a little town like this, everybody knows you. That's a lot of pressure. I've had to ask forgiveness a couple of times. Like a while ago I was paying my utility bill. There was an overcharge, and the woman at the desk didn't understand, even after I explained it to her several times.

I blew up at her. I didn't verbally abuse her, but I can be pretty intense. Well, I went back and apologized, and everything was fine. You just have to be real.

If the church doesn't grow, not just in numbers but spiritually, our denomination has a "turnaround ministry" that we can request. It's for churches where nothing is happening, nothing has been happening, and nothing seems likely to happen soon. The denomination takes over all the assets of the church and assigns new leaders and a pastor.

Financially we could do that. The buildings are paid for, and we meet our budget. We even had a little surplus—about ninety dollars, I think—last year.

Maybe that's what we'll have to do. Spiritually speaking, there are tremendous opportunities here. The sky's the limit. But we have to help people to understand that it's what matters a thousand years from now that's important, not what happens in the next year or two. When you catch a vision of eternity, everything else doesn't amount to much.

Part 4

Splitting
Up

The Bishop
Wanted
a Different
Outreach

11

It's not hard to believe that he played football in college. He's a huge man with a deep voice and a powerful handshake. His bushy beard gives him the look of an Old Testament prophet.

Yet his eyes betray a kindness and gentleness that run deep. His Job-like life has included the severe illnesses of two of his children, and being turned out of a denomination which his family has belonged to and served since its foundation in Europe in the last century.

*   *   *

*M*y dad was a well-known preacher in our denomination, and I expected to stay in the denomination for life, just as he had. The church is connected with where our people come from in the old country, so it's kind of a tradition.

I was called as copastor to a large church in the Midwest, the biggest one our denomination had in a two- or three-state area at the time. We had about eleven hundred people, and soon it grew to seventeen hundred. I felt that my calling was to go out into the community and bring people into fellowship with the Lord.

The senior pastor and I got along very well; I'd have to say that our relationship was marked by love, harmony and unity. He had one role and I had another, and we worked well together. No problems at all.

One year we took forty-two people from our church to a big crusade in another state. That was really something, to see 100,000 people praising God in a sports arena.

When we came back we had a real vision for evangelism, and we sent teams into the community to witness and disciple. The church grew very fast, which I should have realized might cause some friction. There were little signs that I didn't pay enough attention to.

Like what?

People would complain about all the new people sitting in their pews, filling up the classes and such. We grew so fast that people were parking four blocks away to come to classes. Some of the old-timers resented people filling up the parking lot.

But the Spirit of the Lord was moving in me, and it wasn't work; it was fun. It was a thrilling time of life and vitality. Not everyone saw it that way, though. Some of the older, more established people didn't like the changes that growth brought.

The senior pastor resigned, and I was one of five candidates to replace him. It was a time of real blessing. People were praying for us and seeking God's will for my ministry and my family.

Unknown to me, the bishop, who had been a previous pastor of that church, wanted a different outreach. That church was thought of as the plum of the region, and he had different plans. In our denomination there is a strong evangelical group and an older, more mainline group. He resented the evangelical, evangelistic outreach. People had gone to him to orchestrate my removal.

I found this out rather late, and on the night of the big vote there was an electric atmosphere in the sanctuary. People were humming, singing and praying. Even though my future hung in the balance, I sensed God's presence.

I lost by five votes. I found out later that the bishop and his wife had called people and told them to vote against me. Some people who weren't confirmed and some nonmembers voted. There was one re-tarded woman in the congregation who very proudly told people that the bishop's wife had personally called her to tell her how to vote.

I knew that there was more going on there than just an attempt to get me out, though. The church had some very deep problems that did not end when I left.

In the past decade it has had four pastors and three church splits. I felt that night that *I* wasn't leaving the church, but that the glory of the Lord had departed from us in that place.

How did your relationship with people in the church go after you were voted out?

It was a time of wonderful fellowship. We received support from many people who came by to pray, offer financial help and so on. About five hundred people left the church and fed into other churches in the area, so that I had friends in just about every church in town.

A group of four pastors from different denominations came by my house to pray and offer their support. They said, "We don't want to accept any new members without seeing that they are first reconciled to you or the others in the church. We don't want to grow at anyone's expense."

They were very wise. Churches are like a merry-go-round, with people getting offended and jumping off instead of staying on and being reconciled. That hurts the body in the long run, because they take all their resentment along to the new church.

Don't some pastors encourage that by trying to woo people into their churches?

There is a problem with pastoral jealousy. No doubt about it. It's about size and vitality. Some pastors feel a need to have the largest church, or the most vital.

I've learned that vitality is more important than size. I've been in churches with five thousand members and in little fellowships in the oil fields where only six people were present.

I was concerned about vitality, but that made me very visible. Our church became a focal point for the area. We had ranch families driving fifty miles to come to church. Then in the winter they'd worship in small fellowships when they were snowed in. We eventually had twenty-one such fellowships in the area, and it was my job to meet with the leaders.

We had a campaign to get Scriptures in the hands of the people, and we got twenty thousand Scriptures out into the community.

It's surprising that you'd run into opposition over something like that.

It tampers with people's sense of power. One young man, the son of the bishop's closest friend, accepted Christ as Savior. His father was furious with me for praying with his son. "He doesn't need to accept Christ! He's been confirmed!" It was like I'd inducted the boy into a cult or something. Maybe he took it as a criticism of the way he'd raised the boy.

The father's eyes were aflame. *He pauses.* This is something I don't really talk about, but there have been two times that I've seen the devil in people's eyes, and that was one of them. The only other time was at a Billy Graham outreach. I was an usher, and we'd been warned that some Satanists were going to try to storm the platform and harm Billy Graham. We were given a signal to block the aisles and surround Billy, and I could see that the Satanists had been blocked off.

I'm a curious fellow, and I wanted to talk to them, but when I got there they were just spewing hate and venom. I couldn't talk to them.

*   *   *

Churches are like communities. The settlers come in, and then they don't want any more people coming after them. In places like Montana, the settlers don't want Californians coming in and changing things. That's the way some of the old people felt about the church.

In the Midwest particularly, people think of the pastor as a hired gun. They pay him to visit people in their homes and in the hospital. But Ephesians tells us that the work of a minister is to build people up. Early in my ministry I developed the belief that if I was successful I'd work myself out of a job.

If people want a pastor to just attend to their needs, the church will stagnate. If a pastor is building people up, and those people are going out to minister in the community, things will change.

We're seeing in Russia and China where churches thrived in some cases, even though the buildings were closed. The churches that thrived under persecution are the very ones in which the pastors built up the people to carry on the work, not those in which the pastor was paid to cater to a few people's desires.

How did you become aware of your bishop's opposition to your ministry?

One time the senior pastor was gone on a speaking tour, and I had to ghostwrite a paper for him on district evangelism. The bishop asked me, "Did you write that report?"

I said yes, and he just said, "Umm . . ."

He had clashed with the other pastor, and now, I guess, he figured if we were close and in agreement, he'd clash with me too.

After I'd been fired, I was put in a kind of holding pattern with the denomination: "pastor temporarily without call." It was sort of like being on probation or parole. The bishop called me and said that since I was going around praising the Lord after I'd been fired, perhaps I needed to get some psychiatric help.

And not only me, but my wife too! Here's a nursing mother, expected to travel hundreds of miles to the denomination's hospital for psychiatric evaluation because her husband was fired. *Leadership* magazine had an article about pastors' wives. It was titled "The Walking Wounded." Very true.

Did you go?

We really struggled with that. I had worked as an intern chaplain in that hospital, and I knew it wasn't evangelical. I was afraid that it would be a way of stigmatizing me, so I called twelve men I respected—a dentist, a construction worker, they were from a broad spectrum of jobs—and asked their advice.

In Ecclesiastes we're told that there is a time to be silent. This was my time to be silent, so I just listened. All but one said that I shouldn't go, because it was just a trap.

The one who thought I should go said that then I'd be able to say that I'd done everything I was asked to do. But a week later he called and said that after praying about it he'd changed his mind, and he advised me not to go. So I declined.

It's interesting, talking to you about this. Very few people know about this experience, because I just don't talk about it. I don't want to hold a grudge or nurse resentment, so I've committed it to prayer.

Has this whole experience tainted you in the eyes of other congregations? Is that why you're no longer in the denomination of your parents and grandparents?

I was blackballed by the denomination after I refused psychiatric help. The bishop was incensed. He said, "You don't trust me!"

I said, "No, I don't," and he just exploded with anger. He's given me a bad recommendation at every job I've applied for since then, and it's been almost twenty years now.

Back on the night I was fired, a man in the meeting asked the bishop if my being turned down as senior pastor would reflect poorly on my future in the ministry. The bishop said, "Absolutely not." That was a crisp three-dollar bill.

But the same day I came back from telling the bishop that I wouldn't go to the psychiatrist, I got a letter from a well-known evangelist asking me to be a guest for a two-year nationwide evangelistic outreach. How good the Lord is! I headed off to a conference, and what a refreshing time that was.

That was short-lived, though. When I came back from the conference, my wife was not there to meet me at the airport. Friends picked me up and told me that my son was very sick. The doctor thought he had the mumps, and he lanced the swelling but found nothing.

When we got to the hospital, the doctor called me into his private office. That's a bad sign. He told me that they suspected terminal lymphoma, and surgery was set for the following morning.

Here I was, six months after losing my pulpit: I was unemployed, and it looked like I'd lose my son. I thought of Genesis 21—22, where God tested Abraham with Isaac. I said, "Lord, here's my own Isaac." The tumor turned out to be benign.

I can't tell you how difficult a time that was for me, but in some ways it was even harder on my wife. She had even less control than I did, since she had to just watch the process without being in the meetings.

Did you ever feel like just chucking the whole thing and leaving the faith?

No. It was still a time of great blessing. When we did our taxes, we compared the six months in which I'd been unemployed to the previous twelve months in which I'd been drawing a good salary in the church. We actually received more money in the unemployed period. People from all over the world would call or write and tell us that they were praying for us.

Meanwhile, I was still on "temporarily without call" status, and that needed resolving. My not going to the psychiatrist had worked against me.

That brings to mind the Soviet practice of putting dissenters in psychiatric wards: if you disagree, you must be insane.

Well, it wasn't quite that bad. I did have the choice. I could have resigned, but I read about Luther. He did not voluntarily leave the Roman Catholic Church. He was a dissenter, but he didn't want schism.

I was invited to church headquarters in another city for what I thought would be a meeting with a group of six bishops and clergy. This would be my chance to face my accusers and get a fair hearing.

A man in a neighboring church called and told me to go to such-and-such store. I did, and was given a whole new suit of clothes. Right down to shoes and socks. There was a note that said, "It's going to be tough at Headquarters."

That was sure true. I got there to find eighteen people, including representatives of the national headquarters staff. I waited twenty-five minutes for the bishop to present his case, and then I had five minutes.

You weren't present for the bishop's testimony?

No. It wasn't exactly a chance to face my accuser. It was just a formality. In the hotel before the meeting, I read Jesus' words in Mark, where he says, "Don't worry when you are called before the council."

I just went in good faith. I asked if we could pray together. I led. Then I told them that there were three things that informed my theology: Number one, the Bible is the Word of God, the living bedrock foundation for all belief. Number two, Jesus Christ is a living presence in a relationship that grows day by day. And number three, the dynamic presence and power of the Holy Spirit enables me to face an unknown future with a spirit of prayer. That's it.

They spent the next hour and a half on point one. They really had trouble with that. I thought of Luther when he met with the papal nuncio sixty days before the Diet of Worms. Luther said, "I have the Bible on my side and they do not. Popes and councils can err, but my conscience is captive to the Word of God."

Finally, one exasperated bishop said, "You're a pipeline Christian. Everything comes to you directly from God. There's nothing we can do for you." Ten days later, I got a letter saying, "Because of your esoteric grandiosity in assuming that we were not in a posture of prayer..." And that was the end of it. One of the men in that meeting was a golf partner of my dad's. I had gone on a church trip to Europe with a couple of them. But it was over.

My dad went through something similar when I was eight. He was called to see the bishop because he had prayed with people outside our denomination at a Billy Graham-style crusade. He and Mom prayed in the car, and they figured he was going to be defrocked. He wasn't, though.

What did you do after you left the meeting that severed your ties with the denomination?

I drove my rental car around the city. I stopped in a little twenty-four-hour prayer chapel. Then I saw the light of a church, and it was like the pillar of fire in the Old Testament. I just drove there.

The custodian was the only one around, and he and I talked. He listened to me, and we prayed. He was a wise and godly man. He told me about their dream of evangelizing the city and reaching out to all the unsaved. I thought, *That's the kind of pastor I want to be.*

When I came back to town, I was welcomed with open arms by another church. That was a blessed time. One Easter I took a group to the bluffs over the Missouri River, and we prayed for the city. We saw it as God sees it.

I have to work at other jobs—sales, construction, that sort of thing—to pay the bills, but I've been involved in all kinds of ministries since losing my church. I'm one of several police chaplains in this city. I served at a council on family politics where I saw the governor of the state get down on his knees and accept Jesus as Lord.

But my heart's desire is still to be in a pulpit as a pastor. When I came here, I took a pulpit in a fairly new church that had some unresolved problems. I wasn't able to keep that church from splitting, so I went with one group to start a new church.

I was overeager and naive. Starting a new church was a mistake. The people had split over all kinds of unresolved issues that needed to be addressed. That's not a good way to start a new church. The people were not in a posture of forgiveness, repentance or humility. They'd spent too much time battling one another, so every little problem became a big issue.

Here's an example. I was on the pastors' board at my children's school, and one of our church members was behind in his tuition payments, so the school asked me to speak to him. He assured me that he was not behind, but a few days later I saw him at the elders' meeting and he was very upset. "My wife lied to me!" he said. Apparently she had used several thousand dollars for something else, and they were in deep trouble. He resigned from the board so that he could spend time getting his house in order.

His wife was very upset about his having to resign as an elder, and she blamed me. She started talking and then called my old bishop. She got an evil report and spread it all around. That gave her the ammunition she needed, and the place divided up and died. It was terrible. That new church just wasn't in a posture of prayer and reconciliation. It was a battleground.

Do you think that new church might have stayed together if the bishop hadn't given you an evil report?

As I said, that church had been troubled for a long time, but maybe we could have pulled it together. I don't know.

But the bishop has dogged me for a long time now. When I went home to see my mom and dad, I couldn't go to the home church. They were too embarrassed to have a son who wasn't in the family church. I told them that it wasn't my choice, but they're old and very traditional. After my dad died, my mom came out here for Easter. She wanted to know if we'd be worshiping at one of "our" churches.

Have you had any contact over the years with the people who put you out of your denominational church?

I've kept aware. There have been more splits, as I said earlier, and attendance keeps going down. One layman who'd been deeply involved hung himself with piano wire. The policeman who found him said that his head was almost severed. He said that you have to really hate yourself to do something like that.

When my son was in the hospital with the tumor, one of the women who'd been against me was serving as a volunteer. I walked up to her and offered my hand. I said, "I want to be your friend, and I want to ask forgiveness for any harm I've caused you."

She said, "I'll never, never forgive you!" and walked off.

There was one man, though, with whom I did reconcile. When the church officials asked what the charges were against me, he said, "He will never give you a straight answer. He always has to pray about it first."

A couple of years after I left, both his parents were killed in a bad car accident, and he went into a very tough time. I met him at a Billy Graham outreach where we were both ushers.

He said, "You know, if there's one person who is responsible for driving you out of the denomination, it's me. I talked you down whenever I could. Since that time I've come to know the Lord, and I see things differently. I want to ask your forgiveness."

We embraced, right there in that crowded auditorium, and wept together for a long time. We were brothers in the Lord.

Tradition
Was like
a God

12

He's a retired Christian-school teacher whose former students still hold him in high regard. He's a big, strong-looking man with penetrating, almost fierce-looking eyes. But when I talk with him I find that he's a very gentle man.

In his youth he flew bomber missions over Germany. After seminary he pastored in his family's denomination but found it frustrating, which precipitated the move, in midcareer, to teaching.

He's served as a missionary, and he still preaches as a fill-in for pastors who are sick or out of town. He finds that he's in the pulpit nearly every week.

As we begin to talk, I see that despite his age and obvious wisdom, he clearly knows that he has more questions than answers.

*   *   *

I t had been in and out of my mind to enter the ministry for years. Since my teens I figured I'd be a doctor, pastor or teacher. After the Second World War ended I had a wife and kids, so eight or ten years of med school seemed out of the question.

I started college to be a teacher, but I was still weighing the options. Some of my teachers in college, especially one professor who was a converted Roman Catholic, influenced me. He was an Italian from Chicago, which made him kind of stand out in our particular denomination.

He always asked, "Are you doing the right thing?" Then he'd say,

"If you can't hack it, you can always become a teacher." *He laughs.* I don't know what that says about being a teacher.

I didn't stick to a preseminary degree program, because I wanted a different perspective. I took some premed classes, science and so forth. I took history along with the Greek.

Seminary was a good time. I found it helpful to formulate my own thinking—what I believed, what Scripture teaches. Seminary was good for thinking through the basics. I really liked the rap sessions with the guys. There were a few older fellows, and our talks made theology more meaningful than the classes we sat through. Classes did give us the mechanics of exegesis, though. So I was able to learn much more when I finished seminary. But as far as being meaningful, my life experiences were more important. I was thankful for my three years in the service during World War II.

Seminary was a time of reflection and establishing my fundamental beliefs. I used to walk about two miles to school, and I used that time to meditate and think through things. After seminary I learned from reading and from a few good fellow pastors.

I think there are three kinds of pastors. The first kind goes by the book, using all the phrases that will get folks excited. He punches the right buttons, but after you hear one of his rousing sermons you have to ask yourself, "What did he say?"

The second kind tries to be innovative and shock people. He promotes himself. He likes it when people say, "Wow—he's really different." He makes a name for himself. He's really like the first guy, but more clever. He promotes himself and climbs the ladder. He ends up like some of my classmates in seminary—teaching in seminary, pastoring a really big church. But what does he really know? He's got the gift of gab.

The third kind is a people person. He's interested in helping people get through. Sometimes he's a good preacher, but that's not really as important. He can get next to the person in the pew and communicate on a different level. He can communicate about life. He has the basic gift of being a pastor.

You can learn the skills to be a pastor, but that's not the same as having the gift. It's like writing or playing the piano. With hard work anyone can do it, but then there's the person who has the gift. If you have the gift, you have to develop and use it, though. A gifted pastor may never be great in the denominational structure of the church.

The most rewarding thing is to go through the ministry and see that you've helped somebody die with a sense of peace and anticipation. Sometimes somebody will tell me later that I helped them with a crisis in their life, whether it was sickness, brokenness in a relationship, loss of a job, whatever. They come back and say thank you. I appreciate that.

The most frustrating thing about being a pastor is dealing with people who make mountains out of molehills. They fight for the wrong things.

In one church I pastored, tradition was like a god. The elders always sat in the front row of the church. They had always done it that way. Well, a young elder, new at the job, asked if he couldn't just sit with his wife and four kids. The kids were young, and his wife really had her hands full. Those guys really got bent out of shape. "You don't sit with your family," they said. "The elders always sit together in the front row." It was a really big deal to them.

"Okay," I said to them. "We believe in the authority of Scripture, right?"

"You bet," they said.

"Okay," I said, "next time we meet, you show me where it says in the Bible that the elders can't sit with their families."

A few days later we all got together at the regular meeting, and I said, "Okay, let's have it." Silence. "I'm waiting." Silence. "I'm waiting," I said. "Let's resolve this."

Well, one guy said, "We can't find anything directly, but there's gotta be a reason. I just can't come up with it right now."

"So it's the unknown reason," I said. "Like the unknown God in the temple in Greece. Nobody knows, but it's gotta be there."

So they grudgingly said that the young deacon could sit with his wife and children while they researched it. They couldn't just say it was a tradition. On the next Sunday they couldn't even look up at me while I preached. They were worshiping tradition.

*   *   *

People sometimes think you're not a real person. Once I went to dinner at the home of a church family. Later the lady told me that after I left her little girl exclaimed, "Mommy, that man looked just like Pastor Carl!"

Another time I was out for a walk with my wife, and we stopped to chat with a couple of old folks who had a beautiful garden. I was talking to the man while my wife went in the back yard with the woman to look at some flowers. My wife said that the lady was all rattled. "That's Pastor Carl!" she said.

"Yes," my wife said. "That's him."

"What do I say to him?" she asked. "I mean what shall I call him? Reverend? Pastor?"

"Oh," my wife laughed, "just talk to him like you would talk to anyone else."

"Well, that's just what I'll do!" she said.

I wondered why she sort of ambushed me when we came around back. She pumped my hand so hard! They were older folks in a pretty traditional Canadian prairie town, but you get that to some degree everywhere. *He laughs.* She said to my wife, "Just imagine, there's the pastor standing right on my lawn!"

*   *   *

My kids found it kind of hard. They're not passive people, and they didn't like being expected to perform. People wanted them to be part of the package, to always set the example and be perfect.

Once, when they were little, they were playing in our basement. Every kid in the neighborhood was there. It was a pretty warm summer day. I came down to get something, and the whole basement was full of buck-naked children. Every last one of them had stripped down. They were just little kids, but they had that silly grin on their faces. Here I was the pastor, and half the children in the congregation were naked in my basement. I said, as calmly as I could, "What are you doing, kids?"

"We're playing doctor!" They were examining one another, I guess.

I didn't want to make a big deal of it, but I told them it might be good if they got dressed and went outside for a while. Nothing ever came of that little episode, but it was the kind of molehill that could easily have become a pretty big mountain.

*   *   *

I left the pastorate because there were just too many expectations. I ended up working too hard and leaving too many things undone, giving a smattering of attention here and there but not really accomplishing much for all the energy expended. I like to do things well, but you end up fractured and fragmented.

You'd have people whose lives were coming apart. You'd counsel them and say, "Here's what you have to do." Then they'd go out and do just the opposite, as if you'd never even spoken to them.

One gal wanted me to perform her marriage ceremony. Her betrothed was a non-Christian who wanted no part of the faith. I told her, "If you're a Christian and you marry this clown who has no intention of following the Lord, you're just going to set yourself up for a lot of misery."

"Yeah, I know," she said, "But I want to do it anyway."

I told her it was her choice, but I warned her that it wouldn't turn out well. At best all she could hope for was some sort of armistice. I said, "Either you'll leave the faith or you'll have this huge bone of contention between you. There's a remote possibility that he'll join you."

She got really mad at me. Six months later, though, she decided not to go through with it. That didn't happen too often, though.

A lot of times people will become Christians as a ruse to get a guy or gal down the aisle. Then you have to go after them a few months later and say, "Hey, you claim to be a believer," and they just look at you like you're nuts. I had a hard time with those things.

Then a lot of the people in the church spent time harping on things that weren't important, like where the deacons sit. You spend so much time on the unimportant things that you have nothing left for the important ones.

Satan must love to get people to focus on what's not important.

Paul said that we were to press on to the end of the race. It's the end that's important. Not each little step.

*   *   *

When my father died, I had no money to fly to his funeral and the church didn't offer. One guy asked me why I wasn't going. "Is it because of money?" he asked. I said that it was, but he didn't offer to help. If it had been anyone else's father they'd have pitched in. Nobody even seemed to consider that I might be feeling bad. There was no recognition of my grieving. Nothing except a little formal note in the bulletin.

Not every church is like that, though. This was a church without much spiritual sensitivity. They were all part of a tight little community founded by immigrants in the nineteenth century who had come to Canada for the sole purpose of getting rich. They did get rich, but consequently, their relationship to the Lord was pretty nominal. Church was like a social club or institution. Like a lawn bowling club. The church was where you got married, buried and baptized. A good pastor showed up at these three events and stayed out of their lives.

In most churches, especially when the pastor made a lot less money than the people, someone would have offered to help me go to my father's funeral. I've been in churches where someone would have driven me all the way if that was the only option.

But these folks were different. No matter what you preached on, they usually weren't listening. If they were listening, they got mad. One guy came to me and said he wanted to transfer his membership. I said that was okay, but I asked him why. "You get too specific," he told me. "You should stop before you get to that point." There were a lot of them who felt that way. They didn't like anything preached that affected the way they lived their lives. They were just sort of waiting me out, to see when I'd leave. There were a few really fine Christians there, but most of them were pretty cold. So when I was offered a teaching job in a Christian school, I decided to think about it.

Those folks used to say, "Oh, you're from the States. You don't understand us Canadians." The problem probably was that I understood them too well. It had nothing to do with being Canadian or American. That was just an excuse for not listening to the painful truth. I know lots of Canadians, and these people were unique. Humanly speaking, it's an impossible job to pastor a church like that.

It's part of the pastor's job to call people to walk with the Lord. To walk in his ways. But they'd say, "That's an invasion of my privacy." Well, God invades our privacy, and anyone who comes in his name is going to do the same. You can't say to God, "Back away. You're invading my privacy." But they said that I was hired to marry, bury and baptize, not to bother them.

Part 5

Serving
All Faiths

Ministering
to a Transient
Population

13

When I call to ask for an appointment, he is the only one of all my subjects who asks for confirmation from my editor that I'm really writing a book. I wonder if he's going to be a tough interview.

When I arrive on the huge army base, I find him in a small office in the basement of a nondescript building. In a few minutes my fears are put to rest. He's warm, outgoing and humorous. As I watch him field telephone calls and delegate work to his assistants, I realize that the confirmation was not an act of suspicion or paranoia, but part of his normal screening process to keep from being swamped. He's businesslike and very busy.

A captain in his thirties, he's been a chaplain for seven years. He's sharp-eyed, alert and surprisingly open.

*   *   *

*B*ack during the Gulf War, I went into Iraq with an armored division that struck for Baghdad. We didn't know what we'd be in for. We just stormed into Iraq and took a left for the capital.

I'd been in the army as a regular soldier for three years when I got the call, so I'm not just a clergyman with a uniform. I'm an army officer, too.

That invasion was ultimately what the army is all about. The army exists to fight and destroy enemies. That's the world's solution, and it began with Cain and Abel.

I serve the God of peace, and war is not part of God's will. When you have an organization like the army that's built to fight and kill, it sends ripples through the whole organization. There's lots of ways to abuse power and ruin a person's life. I have no illusions about all this. But here I am. I serve gladly, because someone needs to do it. I'd hate to see a military without God's people involved. If we weren't here, it could be pretty bad.

Do you find that some soldiers had a crisis of conscience when it came down to actually having to fight?

Sure. It's one thing to join the army in peacetime. For some guys it's a job, or a way to get money for college. Even the guys who knew intellectually that they were fighting men had to reevaluate when the guns and missiles started letting loose.

Once I was assigned to an armored outfit in Germany. It was one of the tank groups assigned to blunt the first stages of a Soviet invasion, so it was very professional. But even there we felt an unreality. The situation had remained stable for years, and the idea of a shooting war was still pretty abstract.

Also, we were in a defensive position there, so the moral questions were based on fighting if attacked. When our unit was sent to Kuwait, we got ready, then we went charging in. It was more of an offensive situation. There wasn't the idea that it was a strategic stalemate. We were really going to attack and kill. So there was a lot of soul-searching. In the early stages a lot of people had reservations about killing people in that situation. There were thousands of young men, just a few miles across the border, who would soon be dead. And there were some of us who were soon going to be dead.

Everybody gets scared. If a person really says, "Hey, I can't do this!" you have to help them sort through their motivations. If they're just scared, you can get them doing familiar tasks. If they're just plain scared, all the tests of a just war won't do a thing for them. On the other hand, if they're really struggling with the morality of fighting and killing, settling into familiar tasks is not going to help.

I counseled quite a few people, but they all did fine. There weren't any real problems. I had to wrestle with the same questions myself.

I know that there's genuine evil in the world. I know that singing hymns didn't prevent the Nazis from slaughtering the Jews. The slaughtering only stopped when the Nazis were defeated in battle. The state exists as an instrument of God. At its best it protects souls.

As far as serving in a war machine, you don't have to agree with darkness to be a light in it. Now that Desert Storm is all over, I still have no idea why we had to kill 100,000 people over there. It doesn't really make sense to me.

I met with some Russian clergy who are now having to ask these questions. The Russians are talking about instituting a chaplaincy in their military. For the past seventy years it wasn't a question for Russian clergy; technically they were outlawed, so they weren't ever asked to be chaplains. Now they're asking how you can be a chaplain if war is wrong. Remember, they're coming from a country where the historical purpose of the army was to repress their own countrymen. The idea of a military used to protect lives and achieve peace is pretty new to them.

That would be a harder situation—being a chaplain in an army that turned on its own people. I'd really hate to be a chaplain in Ireland, or someplace like that, where historical passions run wild. At least the American soldier doesn't have to be a partisan in wars at home.

What's the typical American soldier like these days?

The military's quite different from the way it was when you were in during Vietnam. There really is a strict policy on drug use. For a while, back in the seventies, they were tolerating a lot of drug use because enlistments were down. Now we're getting a more motivated kind of enlistee, and we don't have to put up with drugs.

Drinking is still a big problem in the military. Some of the guys in the Gulf told me that Desert Storm was the first time in their adult lives that they had been sober for that long. They kind of liked it. It's amazing what a unit is like without all the drinking problems and hangovers. When we came back, though, they just about drank the Enlisted Men's Club dry.

There are still a lot of myths about the military. I heard the news reports that said we couldn't openly worship in Saudi Arabia, but that's not true. Maybe that story was planted in the media to appease hard-liners in the Arab countries, to avoid giving them a propaganda tool. The Saudis considered Christians and Jews to be "people of the Book."

We didn't flaunt our services, but we didn't hide either. We had Communion out in the open. Some of our services were huge. I wrote an "After Action" paper on the subject, and I know that there was no curtailment of religion.

How did you go from being a regular soldier to being a chaplain?

I was called to the ministry in the classic sense. I was in the army at the time, and one night I felt the touch of God. I knew I was being called to the ministry, and then some people in my Bible study suggested I pray about the chaplaincy. I liked being in the army, and it was a good fit.

I served a regular parish for a year and a half while I was in seminary. That was fine and the Lord blessed me there, but I knew that it wasn't what I had been called to do. I knew going into seminary that I'd be back in the army eventually.

The chaplaincy is quite different from civilian ministry. In some ways there's less stress on the family. I have four kids from kindergarten to high school. I know civilian pastors who feel their kids suffer from the PK, or pastor's kid, syndrome. In a civilian church the pastor is in a more public position than a military chaplain is.

The army works on a unit system. Everybody in the unit has a job. My job is chaplain. I'm not the star of the show, and I don't have to depend on the congregation for my paycheck.

I know civilian pastors who really worry about saying or doing something that will result in their being sacked. In some small churches, depending on the denomination, you can offend a key person and you're out. That's stress.

I don't think I could serve in that kind of a situation. My wife has made it clear that she would not. Our denomination doesn't work that way, however. I receive a posting from my bishop.

On the other hand, you are evaluated by a commanding officer who may or may not agree with your goals and beliefs. When part of your job is to be an advocate for the spiritual and emotional welfare of the troops, that means confronting the CO and perhaps telling him things he doesn't want to hear.

For instance, in Germany we had a lockdown during a particularly tense time. Everyone was confined to the base. I guess it's like battle stations on a navy ship. The CO wanted us lean and mean and ready, because there were Warsaw Pact troop maneuvers that were getting a bit too big and close for comfort. The problem was that so many of the troops were married and had their families there in Germany.

The system was developed when the army was made up of single men, so you could just lock down and keep everyone on the line for long periods of time. Now we were keeping husbands and wives away from their spouses and kids. Home life was suffering. Military marriages can get pretty stressed, even with the routine separations and schedule changes. Well, the morale problem got pretty bad, and that doesn't make for a fit fighting unit either.

I had to go head-to-head with the CO over that. It wasn't what he wanted to hear. But the troops were suffering, and it wasn't really necessary to keep them locked down that long. The CO just hadn't noticed the difference from the old days.

Another difference, of course, is that you serve all faiths—not as a pastor, but as a chaplain. That's part of the job. I have to facilitate worship for everyone. I draw the line at assisting Satanism, though.

When I was a regular soldier I met some guys who'd become Satanists in Vietnam. They'd gotten into it for protection. They felt that Satan's power would keep them from harm. It was very pagan. I just stayed away from them.

I haven't run into anyone like that since I've been a chaplain. The closest thing I've seen were some white witches who were in basic training. They were into elemental forces, good magic, stuff like that. They wanted a room to meet in, so I assigned them a prayer room.

Technically, they could have requested use of the chapel, but there's a lot of discretion on my part, too. The chapel is perceived by most people as a Christian building. It just has those connotations.

One time some trainees were marched to the chapel for a cleaning detail. One kid refused to enter the chapel. You can imagine how that went over with the drill sergeant. The kid said, "I worship the devil! I won't enter." I was called to intervene.

I counseled him for several weeks. He was a sad, confused kid who'd been orphaned. He'd been raised a Catholic, and when his folks died he was taken in by people who were Satan worshipers. What it really came down to was that he felt bound by commitments he'd made. As far as he was concerned, he was lost for all eternity and bound for hell.

I explained that no matter what anyone had told him, he couldn't give his soul away, because it wasn't his to give. I explained that God loved him and wanted nothing more than to take him back.

He was pretty unconvinced. All I could do was present the love and the face of Christ to him. There's a time to say that you're damned, but it wasn't his time. He was more confused and afraid than anything. He did finally begin to understand, but then he was transferred and I lost contact with him.

If I was told I had to give a room to outright Satan worshipers or assist them in worshiping Satan, I'd just say no. They'd have to discharge me. I serve at the pleasure of my bishop, and he can ask for me back at any time.

The chaplaincy is a unique ministry. God calls us to twin themes of covenant and service. I made a covenant with the military when I raised my hand and took the oath. I made a covenant with my family when I married my wife, and I made a covenant with my church when I was ordained. But each covenant is made before God. I can't help someone serve Satan.

It's the nature of a fallen world that all of these covenants will exist in tension and conflict. The army could say to me, "You're going to this place or that place." If I felt that it conflicted with my family covenant, I'd have to say no.

As a chaplain you're constantly having to cooperate without compromising. Sometimes I see a new young chaplain's assistant, eager to serve his or her denomination—say the Assemblies of God, or the Baptists. But you have to be just as eager to serve the Lutherans, Methodists and Episcopalians.

I can watch a person for a week and know what denominational "flavor" he has. Some of the young men and women assume I'm not a Christian because I serve people of other faiths. Sometimes they even balk at my serving Christian faiths other than the ones they approve of.

There's a chaplain's assistant who works in our office, a nice young kid, who's appalled that Amy Grant is not singing only gospel music. She just can't see that there is any justification for Amy to sing songs about love or life.

If we're doing our job, we're not making little chaplains. We serve infantry and armored, officers and enlisted. I think that some people don't really understand that the chaplain has a unique job. He's not a pastor, at least not in the normal sense. He pastors Christians, but he acts as chaplain to others, too.

The chaplaincy is a mirror of society. We have about fifteen hundred chaplains drawn from over one hundred denominations. When a denomination gets a certain number of adherents, it gets to supply a chaplain. Jews are the only non-Christian group that provides chaplains right now. The army would consider Mormons Christians. If current trends continue, though, we'll be seeing Buddhist and Islamic chaplains in the next couple of years.

To be accepted as a chaplain, you have to be an ordained minister in good standing with your denomination. Your denomination has to recommend you. In addition, you have to have an M.A. degree, and you have to have experience pastoring a regular congregation.

The question whether I'm a clergyman or a military officer is not as clear as you might think. If my bishop decides I'm needed elsewhere, then he can recall me and off I go. It happens to Catholic chaplains all the time. There aren't enough of them anymore, so they're always getting pulled out. That can be hard if you really see your ministry as being the military.

I'll give you a war story on this. There was a Pentecostal chaplain in Vietnam whose wife unilaterally divorced him. His denomination didn't allow divorced ministers, so it defrocked him. Then, since he was no longer an ordained minister, the army discharged him.

Now, he might have been the best chaplain in the whole army, I don't know. But he lost his wife, his ordination and his army commission in one big blow. They sent him home and that was that.

Anyone who feels he or she is being called to the chaplaincy should ask some specific questions. First, can your family deal with the military lifestyle? Second, can you minister in a truly pluralistic situation? And third, I'd say to look deep inside yourself and ask if you can be a pastor in a situation full of frustration and moral ambiguity.

More than in most other ministries, you work with people for a short time and never see the results. The average length of a personal relationship in the army is one and a half years. That's not much time to disciple. It's a lot different from the experience of a civilian pastor, who might marry a couple, baptize and then confirm their kids, and finally marry their kids.

I Don't Tell Them Where I Live

14

He's a dapper, energetic man in his fifties, short and compact. His clericals are a subtle gray-blue, and he wears a jaunty cap. We meet in a café, not far from the state prison for men.

Somehow I had expected the chaplain for the men's prison to look like a tough cop or a drill sergeant, but he's a bright, dignified, well-spoken man who could be the pastor of an uptown church.

We order a lunch at the counter and move to a window table. I don't know why, but his polite table manners surprise me. He takes small bites and chews quietly. Maybe I expected him to act like the murderers, rapists and thieves he ministers to behind the concrete walls.

*   *   *

I'm the chaplain for the state reformatory. Before that I was an army chaplain for twenty years.

Before I was an army chaplain, I was a parish minister in a large Southern city. That's what drove me into the chaplain corps. There was no pleasing those people! You just couldn't visit enough. And when you visited someone they'd ask if you would visit their cousin or brother or something. The expectations drove me crazy.

My wife could never understand why the parsonage was never private. People liked to have their Bible studies and meetings in the parsonage. One time my wife moved the furniture a bit, and they came and said, "Didn't we always have that chair over there?"

Now they give pastors a parsonage allowance and let them live where they want. I think that's a lot better. A deacon would say to me, "I drove by the parsonage last night. Boy, you had it lit up like a Christmas tree!" What he meant was "We're paying the electricity, so keep the lights turned off!"

In the Army Chaplain Corps they say, "These are the things you're supposed to do." Same with the prison chaplaincy. In the civilian parish you're a fundraiser, an evangelist, a hospital visitor, an administrator, you name it.

Being a prison or military chaplain is also different from being a parish minister in that you have to respect everyone's faith. You can't be denouncing other religions.

My inmate congregation is pretty unchurched, for the most part, but the volunteers bring in prejudices from the outside. They come in and tell the guys that this church or that denomination is a cult. I send word out that while we may not agree on everything, I do not want to hear anyone denounce or condemn from my pulpit. In one service I led the guys in the Apostles' Creed and explained what *catholic* meant. I explained that Christians had shared this belief for 850 years and that *catholic* didn't mean Rome. Then I led an Advent service and tried to show them how Christians share in a lot of basics of the faith.

Our chapel is used by Sunni Muslims, the Nation of Islam, Seventh-day Adventists, Roman Catholics, you name it. I told the guys, "See that beautiful cross that's a permanent fixture in the chapel? If you keep pushing this, we'll have to take that down." The chapel is for everybody. That doesn't mean I believe every religion is the same. No. But I have to do my job, which includes looking out for those other faiths.

I knew a couple of chaplains in the army who came from a very narrow fundamentalist denomination. They didn't last long. They would leave tracts lying around denouncing the Mormons and the Jehovah's Witnesses. They never wanted to share in the services.

In the army you might have a Lutheran chaplain read the Scripture and a Presbyterian serve Communion. Not those guys! They wouldn't water down their faith by sharing with other denominations. They also couldn't stand the cussing and drinking and adultery that go on. I tried to tell them that this was the real world and that it was our job to minister to these guys, to share the gospel with them. But they couldn't get past those things.

*   *   *

As a Protestant chaplain in the prison system you are required to minister to all Christian prisoners, and to facilitate worship for other faiths. Catholics have a different role. The priest is the priest. There are a lot fewer of them, and they mainly work with Catholics.

Yesterday I was dragging two big bags of cedar chips for the Native American sweat-lodge ceremony. Last week I wrote to the Saudi embassy asking for Korans. They sent me a bunch. Now I'm writing to them to see if I can get some prayer rugs.

I know that some ministers would have a problem serving other faiths like that. They'd wonder if they were watering down their witness. But that's what a chaplain does. I'm still me. God is going to ask me on the last day, "Did you take care of my children?" I think I'll be able to say yes.

*   *   *

I'm the only chaplain for seven hundred inmates. We have four contract priests from the Catholic diocese, thirteen volunteer chaplains and three hundred lay volunteers. We have people from pretty much every faith—Pentecostal, Seventh-day Adventist.

There's a lot you don't know about the volunteers. They come and go, and for the most part there's a lack of long-term commitment. It can be pretty hit-or-miss, because there's not a lot of accountability with volunteers.

Working with prisoners is quite different from working with military people, too. You have to be more guarded. You don't let them know about your personal life. I don't tell them about my wife or kids, or where I live.

That's where some of the volunteers get in trouble. We give them classes on working in the prison system. We try to teach them about inmate manipulation.

Manipulation is the hardest thing to get used to. That's why most of the prisoners are here. They're manipulators. They notice *everything!* If I wear a different pin or a new shirt, they notice and ask about it. They just keep trying to get more and more information on you. That's about all they have to do in prison. Especially the guys who are in for a long time. They just keep looking for any angle that will give them an advantage.

It's hard to trust people. You get wary of guys who have gotten "born again." Often it's just a way to get better treatment. You see that when they get out. Some of them just use their faith to get someone to help them out on the outside.

There *are* real conversions. Don't misunderstand me. But some volunteers come in and think they can bypass the system. Some of them just stir things up and get used.

The best way for Christians to help in prison ministries is to work with one of the groups that have been doing it for a while. There are some good groups that help on the inside and on the outside. They establish a long-term relationship that continues when the inmate is released.

They know how to hold the inmates accountable, too. That keeps the manipulators from taking advantage. Some volunteers want to come in and just preach. Some want to develop relationships with prisoners and bypass the system. I can understand that, but it doesn't usually go too well. You just have to be there for the long haul. You have to learn from the people who were doing it long before you came.

Tell the
Parents Their
Son Has Been
Killed

15

Now in his late forties, he's a senior chaplain at one of the largest American air force bases. It's a position of great responsibility, yet his office is in a modest, forties-era bungalow.

He describes his role as being somewhat like that of a bishop. He oversees chaplains, assigns them to new duty stations and implements policy. He's an earnest man, with solid evangelical beliefs and a strong sense of duty.

* * *

*M*y first day as a military chaplain was a baptism by fire. I was ordered to report to my first duty station on a Monday, so I came a day early to attend chapel and see the lay of the land. After the service I introduced myself to the chaplain who was to be my superior.

"Do you have a uniform?" he asked me. I said that I did. "Well," he said, "I really hate to do this to you, but I need you to go and inform a set of parents that their son has been killed."

I got into uniform and drove a hundred miles to see them. Their son was only eighteen. He'd just been in the air force a short time, and he'd drowned.

In those days the chaplain was associated with death. If you came to the door, people knew that their son or husband had died.

Well, I was new to the chaplaincy, but I wasn't new to the clergy. I more or less knew what to do. I contacted the local pastor—fortunately, these folks had a local pastor—and he met me so that we could go together.

When you don't know the family, and they're not really a part of the military, there's only so much you can do. It's different if they're a family that lives on the base, but usually you just walk in out of the blue and announce that their loved one has died.

That must be the hardest part of the job.

It's not easy. I've done it more times than I can count, but I remember every one. The military is good about dealing with death now. The CO goes with a chaplain and a nurse or doctor. That helps, because you never know how a person will respond. I've had people develop chest pains and even pass out. The medical person really helps.

The CO is the one who tells them. Then the chaplain can be there for support.

We have to get there within so many hours to tell them. Then we help them to deal with the remains and get their initial insurance payment taken care of so there's money available for needs that come up. That really helps. We usually get them a check within one day.

I do about ten times as many funerals as a civilian pastor. A lot of them are for retired military personnel who live in the area. There are about forty-five thousand of them in the area, and a lot of them choose a military funeral.

For a person who spent his best twenty years in the service, the ritual is important. The ceremony is very comforting to the widow. The honor guard in their dress uniforms, the flag—it gives a sense that the person is being honored.

When an active service person dies, we help usher the family out of the military. That can be pretty hard for people who have spent a big part of their life with the military. They lose their husband, then their ties are cut off with the military community and the whole routine of life changes.

We also go out to inform parents and spouses when someone dies at a base overseas. That can mean a lot of time on the road. There's no money for chaplains to get a motel. You just get a staff car and go. If you're on the nearest base to the family, you are assigned, so you might have a full day of driving.

*   *   *

The first year I was chaplain at this base we had three major plane crashes. They were big planes—transports—and we lost a lot of people. I went out to inform almost all of the parents and spouses myself.

I was standing at the door of one house at about 6:30 in the morning, and I could see the lady inside washing dishes. The crash had been on the news, and she knew when she saw us why we were there. She wouldn't answer the door. We knocked and knocked, but she just kept washing the dishes.

The law says that you have to wait for them to answer, but finally I just opened the door. The law also says that the CO has to be the one to inform them of the death. It was just so heartbreaking to see the woman standing there ignoring us. The CO was so upset that he froze, and I had to be the one to say it.

Part 6

Staying Open

Never Forget Your Calling

16

He's a displaced Southerner—a priest in a Northern congregation. His boyish good looks and aw-shucks mannerisms belie the fact that he's a graduate of Yale with a mind like a steel trap. As we talk, I find that he's well versed in theology, history and literature. But sitting there in his black clericals and Roman collar, he looks like a good ol' boy who'd be happy talking about fishing at the local café.

*　　　*　　　*

*T*he priest in our denomination is very much like the Roman Catholic priest. We administer the sacraments, conduct the Eucharist and preach. We can also hear confessions and give absolution. It doesn't happen a lot, but when it does, it's a sacred responsibility. We can't divulge anything—even if a crime has been committed.

What if a murderer or child molester confessed?

His penance would have to include confessing to the authorities and paying for what he'd done.

But what if he wouldn't?

I haven't had that happen. Usually when a person confesses to a priest, he or she wants forgiveness and restoration. I would withhold that if the person wasn't willing to really repent.

Some less liturgical Christians would have a big problem with a priest hearing confessions. It might seem arrogant to them.

I can understand that. Actually, the practice of confessing to the priest came out of the biblical injunction to confess your sins one to another. In the early church that just caused a lot of gossip, so the believers decided that the sinner could confess in private to the priest, who would act for the congregation in forgiving and restoring the person.

Doesn't that put the priest above the common believer?

There's a story about Pope John, when he was just a bishop in Italy, that says a lot about the role of a pastor and confessor. John heard that one of his priests was visiting a brothel, so he waited outside the brothel until the priest came out. When the priest saw his bishop waiting for him, he was mortified.

John asked the priest to come with him to the cathedral, and you can imagine that the priest felt like he was in big trouble.

John told the priest to go into the confessional, and he got in the other side. Then John said, "Forgive me, Father, for I have sinned," and he proceeded to let the priest hear his confession.

Then John said, "Don't forget that you're a priest."

Becoming
Transparent

17

This bustling Canadian town is a major shipping port for coal, timber and wheat. A huge pulp mill is one of the town's major employers.

He is a Korean-born Ph.D. who served as an evangelist in one of Canada's largest cities before moving to pastor a small church.

The church was founded in 1907. It met in a tent until the present building was constructed in the twenties. During World War II, when the U.S. Army was in town, the place was packed. Membership had dropped to about twenty-five families when he arrived three years ago. It has now risen to about sixty-five families.

* * *

I know of only one other Korean pastor of a white church. It's pretty unusual. I majored in English literature in Korea, and I came to Canada twenty years ago to live in an English-speaking country. All I knew about English speakers was what I had read in books.

About one hundred years ago, some white missionaries arrived in Korea and planted the seeds of the gospel. They gave everything so that the Korean people could know Christ. They gave their lives. I like to think that I'm giving something back by pastoring a white church.

I've learned since pastoring this church that people are basically the same. The cultural differences are fairly shallow. When you're happy you laugh; when you're hungry you eat. People are pretty much the same.

Being a pastor is very different from being an evangelist. An evangelist preaches most of the time. When you pastor a church, you find out that it's a lot like the world. That can be disappointing.

I liken it to eating in a fine restaurant. You go in and think about how beautiful and tasteful the decor is. You admire the service and relish the food. But if you go back in the kitchen and see how things are run, you might be shocked! That's how it is when you see how a church is run.

When you're a kid in school, or even when you're training to be a minister or evangelist, you have a picture of how the church is. But we're all sinners every day. We make decisions in the church that are not based on the teachings of Jesus but on what's good for us, what we want, what we like.

Jesus taught us to turn the other cheek, but you don't see enough of that attitude among church people. We need to at least turn the other cheek to fellow Christians. If a church doesn't try to follow what Jesus taught, it risks losing its identity. We have to try to do what Jesus did. Church can be pretty political. It can be based on power and position.

I met with a wealthy man who was very important in the community. He was interested in becoming a church member, but one of the first things he asked was whether I could recommend him to be a deacon. This was before he'd even joined the church! I told him that I just couldn't make a decision like that without a lot of time. I'd have to know him for a while. He got rather aggressive when I said that.

In the city we had quite a few Korean churches, and sometimes the ministers—not all the time, though—appointed deacons based on factors other than their Christian walk.

Like what?

Well, if you want to be an elder in a Korean church you have to be a powerful and important person. You might invite fifty or sixty people to your home for dinner. Or if you go with a group to an expensive restaurant, you would pay.

It's not really spoken about too much. It's a cultural holdover, and it's hard for a Korean pastor to break with tradition on this. It's one of those things you have to approach cautiously, or you can stir up a lot of bad feeling.

I'm happy to say that this doesn't seem to be the case in Canadian churches. Financial means aren't as important to Canadians. Really, the people who are humble are supposed to be given responsibility.

*   *   *

What I like most about being a pastor is the joy of being able to introduce people to Jesus and see them receive eternal life. I love to talk to people about Jesus. When I see someone who has never known God, the challenge of helping them come to know him is very satisfying and exciting.

It's challenging because, when you think about it, you're asking people to believe in something they can't see. Without the Holy Spirit, it's really pretty comical. But that's the mystery. It brings me great joy to see God work.

What I find most difficult is that some people don't understand that pastors are humans with limited energy. People seem to expect you to be more than you are. I can get angry, just as Jesus got angry once when he cleansed the temple. I get tired. But when that happens, people are disappointed.

I think they expect perfection because as a pastor you are talking about perfection. If you give a good sermon on love, sacrifice, holiness, when you step down from the pulpit you're expected to be an example of what you just said. How can you meet the ideals you share from the pulpit? People identify you with your speech, but you're talking about ideals for the whole body, not bragging about your own spiritual strength.

Some ministers try to be holier than the rest of the congregation, but I would like to be taken as I am. I don't believe that the minister is better than the people in the congregation.

To deal with those pressures, I repent a lot. I spend a good deal of time in prayer, asking God to create in me a clean spirit. I have to constantly reexamine myself and my attitudes.

Another difficulty is that pastors often have no one they can go to for counsel. I have to admit that I am lonely. I can't talk to people in the congregation as though they were just my friends. I have to keep things to myself.

Sometimes I feel like a garbage receptacle. People come to me and tell me the most awful things. If I carry it all on my shoulders, I can't even get to sleep. So I have to talk to God. Prayer has to be real for me. It can't just be a religious exercise. But I really do feel that I'm talking to God and he's listening.

Still, sometimes you need a friend to laugh with, to joke with. Just to be human with. I have a friend who lives about two hundred kilometers from here. He's Korean, about the same age as me. He's an engineer, and we like to talk because we're interested in many of the same things. Still, I can't confide in him one hundred percent.

Two hundred kilometers is a fair distance. Don't you have any other close friends?

I have another friend I've known since high school. I can be one hundred percent open with him. We sometimes talk in the language of high school. He's a professor in a big university in the prairies, so he's even farther away. We phone and write to each other.

He holds a very high position in the academic world, so he likes to kick back and talk with me. We both benefit from our relationship.

Do you think that friends from long ago are generally more willing to let you be yourself instead of The Pastor?

Sometimes. But in 1980 I went back to Korea and met some old friends, and we had grown apart. Our educational level was different, and we had lived different lives. There were too many gaps.

I do have friends in the congregation. Most of the people are working-class, but there's a teacher, a publisher and an editor, so I do have some intellectuals to talk to here. I find that people with similar educations are easier to talk to.

I have to say that I'm somewhat skeptical about my attitude toward openness. I did have one experience where I was open with a person in the congregation and then word got around. Then it got distorted and caused a lot of trouble. That made me become more wary and cautious.

But as I say, I'm skeptical about my caution. Jesus wasn't always watching what he said or to whom he said it.

I think that our fear of being open comes from our lack of confidence in our own integrity. If I really believe in myself, why should I worry about people getting to know me? I would like to become bold enough to let people really know me. But to do that I have to be consistent in my beliefs and in my life.

It's like cutting open an apple. If that apple is good all the way through, it need not be ashamed to be opened. There's no corruption inside. But if there is corruption inside, it won't want to be opened.

But if we wait until we're clean through and through, won't we have a pretty long wait?

That's true. I guess I'm not making myself clear. As I said, I'm thinking my way through this question. You know, the best philosophers are willing to say, "I don't know," if they don't have the answer. We pastors have a hard time saying that, because people expect us to have all the answers.

That's where we miss something of what Jesus came for. I remember a church in Montreal where a woman came to join the choir. Later, the choir people found out that she'd deserted her husband in another town, so they kicked her out of the choir. But were they themselves that good?

Jesus didn't come for the righteous; he came for the sick and the unclean. I hope that someday I can feel confident enough about who I am, and secure enough in Christ's love, to be boldly open about myself. To let people know me as I am.

When My
Wife Left,
It Was Not
a Surprise

18

He's a gentle, athletic man in his forties. He serves in a large church with several other associate pastors. Each has his or her specific area of ministry.

In the pulpit he is very warm and easygoing. Up close I can see that he is also an intense, hard-driving professional, which surprises me a bit.

He's tired when we meet; it's probably not the best day for an interview. But we chat for a few moments and begin talking about the most painful event in his life.

* * *

When my wife left me, it was not a surprise. She had been going through therapy for several months when she told me she had a secret to share. She had been involved in a relationship with a woman for seven years. That relationship was breaking up, and she was on the verge of another one.

I felt, sad, angry, guilty, depressed—all those feelings. It was hard on me, on the kids, on my wife. We had started off in ministry together. She'd felt the call as much as I had. Then the drift had begun.

People in the congregation had *sympathy* for me but not *empathy.* I got a lot of help from the staff, and I participated in Divorce Recovery Workshop at our church. The ministry reaches out all over the city, so I was able to fit in and not immediately tell people what I did for a living. One guy said, "I like this place. You ever come here, John?" I said, "Sure, I come here a lot."

*   *   *

Most people in this church know that under the collar we're the same as anyone else. Out on the street it's not that way, though. Telling the gas station attendant or a kid's new teacher that you're a pastor can be hard, because they often have such stereotypes.

Someone has said, "The good news is that we're all bad." Jim Bakker and Jimmy Swaggart shouldn't be news to us. Their behavior was bad, as it would be in any profession. It shouldn't happen, but it does.

If we were really doing our job in the church, no one would be surprised by Bakker and Swaggart. They would already know.

Anything is possible. Nobody should say, "That won't happen to me. I won't get divorced, get cancer, have a kid on drugs." The more you try to avoid something, the more likely it is to happen to you. I'm not saying that you should put yourself in tempting situations. Not at all. But denying the possibility is a good way to get into trouble.

I face that all the time when I counsel. Counseling is a good way to get in trouble if you have the attitude that it can't happen to you. You have to do the sensible things. Leave the door open sometimes. Don't go to a single woman's home to counsel.

I don't counsel anyone more than seven times in a row. Six or seven. If we aren't making progress by that time, the person needs to see someone else. I usually ask them how they think things are going, if they're still growing, what responsibilities they feel they have to make things change.

I'm a pastor, not a counselor. We have many excellent counselors, therapists and psychologists in the congregation. Their job is to treat people, sometimes medically, with drugs. I can't really treat people. I can simply be their pastor.

Sometimes I have insights that can make a significant impact. Simple things: Say thanks, or please. Ask. Say what you need. Don't hide grudges. Trade initiatives. Sometimes we get in roles of pursuer and distancer; trade roles for a while. Flip a coin. Sometimes simple things make a big difference.

I don't mind counseling people sometimes, but my role as a pastor is to empower other people to minister. My greatest pleasure as a pastor is when I can say, "I don't have to do it; the church has done it."

Today I went to see a lady who had a massive stroke last night. When I was at the hospital, a note signed by the four deacons from her area came. One of the deacons had been with the family last night. They got there before me. So if I fail, it's not the end of the world.

I love doing weddings, baptisms. Promises are made and hope is held out. The promise of new life reflects the promise of the gospel. But even doing marriages can be a sad affair. Sometimes I have to say no to a couple that shouldn't get married. That's hard, but it's not as hard as marrying people who are going to tear each other up.

If, as a pastor, you try to take on everyone's pain, you can get burned out. That's why it's so important to empower and enable others in the congregation to do the work.

We get ourselves in pretty deep sometimes. Sometimes a person will tell me something really disturbing or shocking. It's hard to learn to maintain a distance, to avoid being shocked.

What do I do when someone tells me something really shocking? Sometimes I just fall apart, but I try to see it as human.

Maintaining
the Standards
of a Holy
God

19

The little white church and parsonage were built by Scandinavian immigrants in the last century. They are snuggled in a lovely community of modest homes and farms.

I enter and find that the table is already set. I have been invited to dinner— a wonderful treat when you're on the road, a welcome break from fast food and diners.

A little boy greets me by shooting me with a toy pistol, while another child peers shyly from around a corner.

The pastor welcomes me and we retire to his study, which is small and packed with books. He has the scholarly manner of a college professor and the friendly warmth of a country parson.

As we begin to talk, I see that he also has the forcefulness of a debater. He's a man of strong convictions—convictions he can back up with logic, rhetoric and Scripture.

* * *

*T*he pastorate is becoming nothing more than another profession. It's not seen as a calling or gifting anymore. Future pastors are trained in family counseling and all kinds of personal growth courses. There aren't as many true believers in the pulpit any more.

He hands me a letter, written by him to the local ministers' council, informing them that he can no longer be a part of their fellowship.

It was hard to break with the Ministers' Council over the issue of homosexuality, but their stand was so blatantly unbiblical I felt that I had no choice. I'm the only pastor in this community who believes that homosexuality is a sin rather than an alternate lifestyle. And if anyone says I don't understand the issue, my second son was involved in homosexuality before he died. I know what's involved, believe me. It's hard, in a way, to take a stand when everyone else sees it differently. I try to remember that at one point in history, after the execution of John the Baptist, there was only one man on earth who had the truth: Jesus Christ.

Christianity has moved from being a religion based on absolute, concrete truth as its basis of faith, to a relativistic religion. I sat in a Ministers' Council meeting where a pastor from a cult prayed over the meeting. His prayer was a cult prayer, but the minister next to me said, "What a wonderful prayer!"

Pastors are supposed to be shepherds and spiritual leaders of the flock. Too many people profess Christ but don't know anything about the absolutes that have stood for eighteen hundred years. If you ask people today what the main attribute of God is, they'll probably tell you it's love. It's *holiness*. "Holy, holy, holy," says the Scripture. How can we trust God's love unless he is a holy God? And if he is holy, then he will demand perfect love and perfect justice.

The liberals of the nineteenth century lost the concept of God's holiness. I asked the ministers in the council, "When is the Word not the Word, then? When does it not mean what it says?" They all had a different answer.

If you say the Word errs, you are saying God errs. I seem to be the only one in this community who will say that. They say I'm too rigid and unloving, but everyone has standards. Mine just happen to be the ones I read in the Word. They would all draw the line somewhere—child pornography, perhaps—but they won't just read the Word.

It frightens me. A Christian should be able to name ten basics of the faith. There was a time when every believer knew the basics of the faith. That was the norm. I'm not trying to judge people, but I can't be associated with people who know the truth and deliberately teach something else. That's hard sometimes.

There was a woman whose husband was ill. For four years I was the only one to enter their door. She took on membership here and started walking with the Lord. When her husband died, she wanted me to do the funeral service. But she wanted it in that church building where he had been a nominal member before. I had to say no because of the position I'd taken in breaking with those ministers. I felt terrible. In her moment of greatest trauma I couldn't do it.

The director of the funeral parlor was furious with me. He said, quite indignantly, "I just don't understand this kind of behavior!"

But what do you do? Do you say, "We'll accept this one sin?" You can't join Christ to a harlot.

I came to this church four years ago and started teaching from Ephesians. Forty percent of the members walked away. Then they tried to get rid of me because of what I was teaching. I'd show them Scripture and they'd say, "I don't believe that."

I taught from John and then Romans. Romans has just about every doctrine in the faith. And some people appreciated the teaching.

New people started coming, and now we're larger than before. But it was painful. The church is growing and thriving, but a lot of people in this community dislike me. I don't mind, but it's hard on my wife. You can feel the tension. Sometimes she's gone into a store and people would just walk to the other end of the store and wait until she left. She developed psoriasis from the tension she felt.

People have said, "You have a nice family. Your daughter has such fine Christian character. It's too bad you're so rigid." I wonder if they can connect my daughter's character with what she has been taught all her life.

People can be so unreasonable. We had a really tight vote over one issue, and a fellow asked, "Is your wife going to vote? That's not fair!" I told him that she was a member of the church just like us and she could vote if she felt like it.

*   *   *

There have been some real joys though. There were two men working in a mill near here. They got into a fight on the job, and one injured the other. The injured man couldn't work for a while, so the other man was promoted to a job that the injured man had been in line for. Both of them had problems with alcoholism. Their marriages were in trouble. They had terrible tempers. Anyway, they both started coming to church, and the one who had injured the other fellow sought counseling. One Sunday, kneeling at the Communion rail, he asked forgiveness from the man he'd injured. Now they're brothers in the Lord.

As we teach the truth and hold Christ up, people can see the difference. When we teach truth we glorify Christ. He makes the difference, but you have to believe his Word.

A man in the church lost his wife. She just walked out on him and began living with another man. He told her that he loved her and that the door was open. It was Hosea all over again. He had a lot of growing to do, but in Christ it was possible.

I've done funerals, though, where the resentment was so strong that people stood in the back with their hands in their pockets. I've had to grow to accept this.

One couple, who'd grown in the Lord, wanted a Christian wedding. They specifically invited nonbelievers. I preached on a bride for Isaac and Christ's love for the church. After the service, some women told me I was a chauvinist. I'd just quoted the Word. The greatest problem since the Fall is that people ask, "Did God really say that?" That's what the serpent said to Eve.

I see my job as being here to teach for the equipping of the saints. Servanthood is a lost ideal, but we're told that we should come out of our bondage to sin and enter a bond of love with Christ Jesus.

*   *   *

I felt a call to be a pastor when I was in high school. Then I saw what it took to be a pastor—a true pastor, that is—and I ran for twenty years. The Lord had to get my attention, and it cost me dearly. I was disabled on the job, which left me in constant pain for the rest of my life. I couldn't get insurance, because the employer disclaimed my injury. I had no income, and then my sixteen-year-old son died. His older brother ran away from home, blaming me for his brother's death.

I said, "I quit, Lord. Where do you want me to go?" I was at the end of my endurance. My son's death was required for me to stop and listen to the Lord's call. Now I understand crucifixion.

The older son, who was seventeen, had a terrible time. He was using drugs, listening to heavy metal. The whole feeling in the home was charged with anger and rebellion. He had no job, but he got a car with promises and a handshake from a friend of mine. I didn't know about this deal at the time. He had no insurance, and within a few days he'd totaled the car. I paid it off by trading it with my friend for some guns. I had been a police officer for a while, so I had several guns.

The tension was even worse after that. He wouldn't pray with the family; he just walked out. He still blamed me for his brother's death.

How did his brother die?

He shot himself. He used my gun. People asked me how I could keep the gun after that. Guns don't kill people. Someone has to pull the trigger. I was at a mission at the time. He lived for a little while. It wasn't a clean kill. He died in my neighbor's arms before the aid car got there. The last thing he said was, "Tell Dad I'm sorry. Tell him I love him."

Were the two boys close?

Oh, they had their disagreements, but yes, they were pretty close. Like normal brothers.

Things kept getting worse. The older brother got another car and wrecked it in a matter of a few weeks. I found myself thinking, "I almost hate this boy! Why?" And then I realized it. It was as if the Lord had said, "It's because he is not mine."

I told my wife to go away for a while, and then I had a talk with my son. I said, "You hate us. Well, you have two options. You can stop using drugs, get rid of the heavy metal and be a part of the family, or you can leave. You have five minutes to decide." Five minutes later I told him, "Out now!"

That was excruciating. Sobbing, I said to him, "I'm going to ask the Lord, 'If my son is not yours, do whatever it takes to make him yours. If he is yours, please take his life, because it's a disgrace the way he's living now.' "

A few weeks later, a few of his druggie friends came around. They said they were worried because they didn't know where he was and nobody had seen him for a while. It turned out that he and another kid were racing, and my son drove his car off a big bank and crashed. The other kid had a rap sheet, so he took off. He was afraid that he'd get in trouble if the police found him connected with a car crash.

My son's car had rolled down the hill, and he was thrown out. He was lying in the bushes unconscious, with a broken leg and glass in his back where he'd gone through the windshield.

The doctors said they couldn't operate because they didn't know what kinds of drugs he was on. They ended up putting a steel pin in his leg.

He woke up later and I saw him. He said, "God could kill me!"

I said, "I want you saved, not dead!" The day before his eighteenth birthday, the day before he got out of the hospital, he was saved. He became a new creature in Christ. He got work and bought auto insurance—which was hard, since he'd totaled three cars in ninety days. He married a Christian girl, and they've had three kids.

When we found out that my wife was pregnant with another child, we were surprised—and happy. When the baby was born, my oldest son said, "I know he can't take John's place, Dad, but I'm glad it's a boy."

How is your oldest son doing now?

I haven't seen him in a year. He was doing well, but then he started backsliding. He left his wife and just took off. I asked him, "What is it that you want?" Silence. He couldn't say anything. The last thing I said to him was, "When you and Christ are walking together, then you and I will be able to walk together."

* * *

A life in the ministry can be horribly painful. It's a privilege and a joy, but there's also pain. Before anyone enters the ministry he should ask: *Am I sure I'm called and gifted?* It's not just a profession. You can't learn to be a good pastor. God gifts you.

Be prepared to do a great deal of praying and crying. Be vulnerable, because you are vulnerable. You'll hurt when your sheep hurt.

The pastor is the only one outside of blood relations who goes from birth to the grave with you. He baptizes you and marries you.

Christ went looking for the sheep that was missing. So often you hear people say, "I've been gone for two months and nobody's called." A shepherd has to know his sheep.

Christ said to fast, pray and read the Word of God. It's like one of those three-cylinder cars. If one of the cylinders isn't firing, it's going to be pretty bumpy. Go to the Book. The Book remains correct.

Be available, even when you don't feel like it. Your hours won't be your own. I was studying for my sermon the other day when an old man dropped in. His dog had died. That dog had been his one true companion for eighteen years, and he was devastated.

You have to listen. Be sensitive as to how you listen, because often it's what's left unsaid that is the key, not what is said.

Part 7

Bearing Burdens

Their Biggest
Need Is What
I Was Instructed
to Ignore

20

The pastoral ministry class at his Bible college is populated mostly with fresh-faced teenagers. At twenty-six, this former drug and alcohol abuser stands out. He has the intense, world-weary look of a man who has taken a few trips around the block. His faith is his own, not something inherited from his parents. He was raised a nominal Catholic, and after a serious motorcycle accident, he decided to change his life.

He signed up to train for a charismatic Catholic evangelistic team, without really knowing what evangelism was. When asked if he had a problem with tongues, he replied no. How else would one talk? he wondered. The same with visions. "Everybody has visions," he said, thinking his questioners meant eyesight.

A week and a half into the training he met Christ, and now he is studying to be a youth pastor in a Protestant denomination.

*   *   *

*M*y degree will be in youth ministry, and then I'd like to be a youth pastor. I have had a year of experience as a youth pastor, in a small rural congregation. The church had just undergone a major split, with about half the congregation following a deacon out the door. The pastor told me in the interview that there had been a split, but that it was "no big deal."

Well, it *was* a big deal. A very big deal. It was a small town, and a lot of people gathered in the café for coffee and conversation. When I went in there, people started cursing me. They'd say, "There's that

S.O.B. who took the youth pastor job at the church."

I walked over to some of them and said, "Hello, my name is Chuck. I don't know you . . ."

They sneered and said, "We know who *you* are. And you must be as crazy as that S.O.B. pastor if you can work for him!"

I mean, it was vicious. I found out that one of the couples who had helped engineer the church split owned the café, so it was kind of their hideout. I tried to talk with them, but it was like I was an enemy spy or something. I found another place to take my coffee.

I told one of my professors about that incident, and he just said, "Well, you've learned something about developing the tough skin of a pastor." He wasn't all that surprised.

The pressure of the split was on my pastor. People called him at home, and they cursed him when he went out, too. We'd have staff meetings once a week, just the two of us, and he'd vent all his frustration on me. I guess he couldn't talk about it at home, because his wife was taking it pretty hard. He really needed some professional counseling to work things out. When I'd try to talk with him, he'd just clam up and say it was best to let it go. But he couldn't let it go. It was really eating him up.

His kids were pretty soured by the experience. His daughter, who had just graduated from high school, insisted that she would never marry a pastor. She was emphatic. She said she could never put her family through what her parents and brother were going through.

I think she had a pretty healthy perspective on it, in spite of her disgust with the situation. She had a strong personal faith, and I expect that she'll be okay. The younger brother is the one I worry about. He was more quiet and moody. I think he took a lot of heat at school and in the little community.

It was a tough year for me, too. We didn't agree fully on a philosophy of youth ministry. Partly that was because of age. I'm twenty-six and he's fifty. I was learning youth ministry in a more contemporary way, whereas he was of the old school. He was a great guy to learn from, though. I appreciated him.

But the kids had been deeply hurt by the split because it separated friends. One family stays, the other leaves, and the kids are pulled away from their friends in the church. That's a tough thing to do to kids when you're trying to teach them to develop a Christian community among themselves. Some of the kids were very cynical about the split—just like kids whose parents are divorcing. They felt that the adults were too immature to resolve their differences, and it all came down hard on the kids. Just as in a divorce, the kids were expected to choose a side, when all they wanted was restoration. Their lives were impacted negatively, but they had no power to make things better. They just had to stand by and watch their lives crumble around them.

I wanted to pastor the kids through their grief and loss and give them some hope, but the pastor said not to talk about it. He laid it out for me, but told me not to discuss it with the kids.

Everybody in town was talking about the split—mostly in a destructive way. I wanted to help the kids work through their feelings and look to the Scriptures. But I had to just leave it alone. It was their big need, and it was the one thing I was instructed to ignore.

There were only about three kids there the week I started. We built it up to fifteen or twenty-five who were from the church, and then went out to the unchurched. But there were some open wounds that weren't being healed, and that colored the whole atmosphere.

I'm not sure I'd have taken that job if I'd known about the animosity in the community and the pastor's denial. Maybe it was good for me to come in not knowing, but I should have been able to provide healing once I was on staff. I saw my job as supporting the pastor. I think a youth pastor should be there for the youth, and also to make the pastor a hero in their eyes. You want to give the kids a sense of belonging, so that they can grow into leadership in the church.

After a while I began to think that maybe it wasn't all the deacon's fault. It was definitely over power—who controlled things. But I saw pride in the pastor, too. He had the "my church" attitude: "I'm the pastor. You're not. I'm the shepherd. You're not."

I wish we could have all sat down together in a spirit of prayer, but it just didn't happen. There was no interest on anyone's part—except maybe some of the kids—in reconciliation. Everybody had to be right.

The stress from that job spilled over into other parts of my life. I'm a resident assistant on a dorm floor. It's kind of like being the pastor of the floor. That can be fairly stressful, especially when you're planning a wedding in a few weeks.

One night at 2:00 a.m. I blew up at some guys who were being noisy. I really let them have it. The next day there was a note on my door that said, very politely: "Next time, maybe you should think before you speak."

I was furious. I wanted to find out who had the gall to leave an anonymous note criticizing me! Then I prayed about it, and I could see the similarities to the situation at church. I wanted to be right. I wanted those guys to be wrong. And I wanted everybody to agree.

Finally, a job opened up closer to home. I was driving over an hour each way to that job, so working closer to home began to look like a good idea. The time and the stress were dragging me down.

Besides developing a tough skin, I can see now that any pastoral role is going to require a genuine call and a lot of maturity. Some of the ministerial students on this campus are seventeen years old, and they are planning to be pastors. A surprising number are here because their fathers are pastors.

One friend of mine is the son of a prominent preacher in our denomination. He's got a degree in pastoral studies, but he's afraid to preach. In homiletics class he actually passed out when he had to give a sermon. Now he's back in his hometown working at Burger King. I don't see how he can ever be in a pulpit.

I feel a real call, but that came to me in the course of my life. There are a lot of people here who have a real call, and there are others you have to wonder about.

Actually, the pastor I served under is also the son of a well-respected preacher.

*   *   *

I didn't know it then, but one of the deacons resigned the same day I did. There were five board members at the time of the split. Two were totally for the pastor, and the others resigned. The bylaws required no fewer than five board members, so they tried to change the rules to no *more* than five. Well, you just can't do that. But they couldn't find qualified board members. I think the church is down to about forty members now. It was around 320. It's not getting any better.

I know how hard it must be for the pastor, but I think he needs to take a sabbatical or leave. His name is mud in that town, and I don't see how he can minister to those people anymore. He needs to get out, and they need a pastor and a deacon board with a vision to rebuild. Right now there's no vision. He's just holding on, and the church is dying.

I hope to attend that church this summer, after I'm married. Maybe a few of us can have lunch together. Now that I'm not a member of the staff, perhaps I can help him to focus on what he can do. I'm not too hopeful, because he's just trying to hang on, and he's not interested in doing anything innovative.

The last seven words of a dying church are "We've never done it that way before." The church is always one generation away from extinction, and I saw that principle in action. That's why I want to be a youth pastor. The youth are the ones who carry on.

Let My
People
Grow

21

He's a nationally known leader, the author of several well-reviewed books, and presently the chairman of a Christian community-building ministry in the African-American area of a large city. He's often asked to speak at national conventions. We agree to meet for breakfast at seven the following morning.

When I arrive at his home/headquarters in a modest, working-class neighborhood, he is sitting in his office, wearing an old bathrobe. He's consulting with a lawyer and an accountant, both of whom seem to know him on a personal basis. His wife comes in and sees the two men in suits and me. She's dressed for the day, and she shakes her head as she looks at his bare legs sticking out of the beat-up bathrobe. She turns away without saying anything and walks back out. "It's OK, honey," he calls after her, "we're all friends here."

She laughs, letting us know that she's not mad, just embarrassed. She's a Southerner, not prissy, but with a sense of decorum that he lacks. She wouldn't receive visitors in her bathrobe.

He looks over a stack of spreadsheets and then excuses himself to dress. In ten minutes he returns, and we're off to a local restaurant for breakfast. It's the only way he can escape the constant stream of visitors and phone calls.

*   *   *

T he urban family is in big trouble now, because the whole idea of family, which comes from God, is all messed up. Back in Africa black people lived by family. The village was just an extended form of family, with the chief and other leaders like fathers. It wasn't perfect, but it was pretty close in some ways to God's model. When black folks were uprooted and brought over here, family was deliberately crushed. We're still feeling the pain. In a lot of ways it's getting worse.

Communities and neighborhoods in this country are pretty unstable. We (black people) have only lived in this neighborhood here for twenty years. We replaced the whites. Now the Hispanics are replacing us. Everybody keeps getting moved. There's no sense of belonging.

We respond to noise. When something big happens, we want more police or a new program. But what's needed is family and community. You talk to some of the young people in this neighborhood, and you know how lost they are. How unconnected they are.

I hang out on the corner sometimes, just to see what the young guys are thinking about. There's a liquor store right across the street, and the young guys just congregate over there. Some of them know I'm a preacher, but some of them don't, so they just talk freely as if I was just one of the guys. I get so full of despair listening to them that I could see how someone might just get an AK-47 and go mow them all down. The big thing now is to make girls give them oral sex for drugs. They feel a tremendous need to humiliate and use women. One guy was bragging that his dope blew this girl's mind. *Bragging!* She took some of his dope and now she's in a psycho ward, and that makes him a big man. How do you even begin to build families and communities with those guys?

I put my little granddaughters on the plane back to their parents the other day. They're cute little girls, just entering their teens, developing women's figures and all pretty. What would I do if one of those guys gave my granddaughters dope? Or got one of them pregnant? It's hard to love everyone like you're supposed to. It's hard to go on sometimes when things just seem to be falling apart faster and faster. But getting rid of those young men won't help anything.

There's got to be someplace for them to go. They need to accept Christ, but then they need to be discipled—in some very basic things.

Usually when I talk about this to well-meaning white people, they say, "Oh, well our neighborhoods are just as bad." What's that supposed to mean? It's like they're saying, "Why are you so upset?"

I went and saw that movie *Boyz 'N the Hood* the other night. It was pretty accurate in some ways, like how it is with young black men in the neighborhoods. The anger, the frustration, the sense of going nowhere. But how did it end? Out of that whole bunch, two kids made it. And how did they make it? By getting accepted to Howard and Morehouse colleges! That's great, but I bet those colleges don't take more than three or four hundred freshmen a year. There's more kids than that right in this neighborhood. They can't all go to high-priced colleges, and they know it! There's a lot of despair.

* * *

White people run Congress. Black people think if they put more money into it they can have access, but it doesn't work that way.

A lot of black leaders, especially young ones, think that I can get money and the ear of congressional representatives for them. They see me meeting with those people (congressmen) and they assume I'm well off and connected. They get mad when I don't go to all of their meetings or exercise my supposed power on behalf of their plans.

But the politicians get nervous when I'm around. They're afraid that I might replace them, so I've backed off politics. I just advise now. I don't let them think that I'm out for their jobs.

Unfortunately, I don't get along well with most of the preachers. I don't like preachers. *He laughs.* They display too many false airs. They're so worried about coming across like the preacher that their true personality doesn't come out. They're too uniform. Being a Christian should enhance a person's true self, but mostly, being a preacher *dehances* it.

When God truly molds us, he molds us into something unique and beautiful. He doesn't make us into somebody else. But most preachers are in a straitjacket mold, and they end up putting other people in that same mold.

People seem to seek you out because you empower them rather than put them in a mold. How does your family deal with all the visitors?

My wife gets worried and angry. It's good and bad to have the office in the house. There's always faxes and phone calls and visitors. But on the other hand, if I can't sleep I can get up and work.

* * *

A lot of leaders, especially leaders in the black community, want me to anoint them with "the Power." When I don't anoint them, they feel empty, and they put their energy into disappointment.

I have a love-hate relationship with one particular young man, just like a father and a son. He wants me to move out of the way and anoint him. When he struggles in his ministry, he feels that I'm withholding my blessing on him—as if there were something else I could do to make his job easier. He says, "You could really make it happen for me!"

I'm a simple man. There's nothing mysterious about me. I look in the mirror and I don't see a genius. A lot of my ability to motivate people comes from being able to say things clearly. I never did have much schooling, just a few years in grade school. Maybe that's why I can restate things clearly. I can take something and reword it so that the average person can say, "I understand that!" That's my gift if I have one.

But there's nothing special about me. People see all my degrees on the wall (he has several honorary doctorates) and say, "How'd you get those?" They want me to show them how they can get some degrees. I tell them, "They just *gave* those degrees to me!"

In the black community there are a lot of churches that just about belong to the pastor. The pastor is the church, and when he gets old he grooms his son to take over for him. Maybe that's why people expect me to anoint them.

*   *   *

The major disappointment white people feel about me, and I think about all blacks, is that we don't love them. They think in their minds, "After all I done for him, that nigger has the gall not to love me!" White people can be pretty paternal. They think that if they help you out, it'll erase centuries of oppression and bad feelings. I'm not saying I hold a grudge, but I don't just love anybody right off who helps me out—especially when they're just doing what they're supposed to. But they get mad if I don't love them!

Look at those people out there on the green. *He points out the window to a nearby golf course.* Those guys, I don't know if they're

Christian or not, but they couldn't care less that I'm in here eating in the same restaurant with white people. But their lack of opposition is not a favor to me. That's just how it's supposed to be. It wasn't always like this, especially down South where I'm from, but the "progress" that makes it okay for me to eat here isn't some favor, it's just simple dignity.

This country has come a long way. The overt racism that I grew up in—separate schools, segregated public facilities—that's a thing of the past pretty much. But black people are still lagging. I think that all the welfare grants and public housing and so on were good, but they weren't meant to be permanent. They were just meant to be a temporary way to let us catch up. It bothers me, though, that some of the people who fought those entitlements every step of the way are now saying so happily, "See. It didn't work, so let's scrap it!"

The extent to which those programs have worked for some people is through no help from the naysayers. Maybe those programs would have worked better if they hadn't been fought every step of the way. Maybe not. I guess we'll never know.

Don't Deny
My People's
Pain

22

The winter months are tough in this logging community. Logging, besides being one of the three most dangerous jobs in the country (the other two are fishing and farming), is seasonal. But the federal government has banned logging of old-growth timber, partly to protect the habitat of the spotted owl. The result is that families have been thrown out of work, expensive equipment has been rendered worthless, and the major source of income for the entire area has been eliminated. The financial outlook is gloomier than it's ever been here.

We meet in her office, which also serves as the church's nursery school. Lilliputian chairs and table take up half of the room. The phone rings; a fellowship for retired people is setting up for a coffee hour in the next room.

Every pastor has a special focus. For some it's evangelism, for others discipleship. In this congregation it's trying to keep the fabric of the community from unraveling. The people of this Northwestern town are tough. Nobody expects a free ride, but this last blow is just too much, and despair threatens to take over the lives of the people.

She spreads a half-dozen issues of the local newspaper on the low table for me to look at. Banner headlines predict doom for the one-industry area.

*   *   *

We served seven years as copastors, but I resigned this month to minister full-time to people who are out of work because of the spotted owl decision. My husband is still the full-time pastor.

We started seeing timber-related headlines about two years ago. When timber slumps, the whole area goes into a tailspin. It's so important to these folks that it took up a whole congregational meeting.

It's the thing everybody talks about. That's when we decided to put together a task force. We invited other pastors to come and talk about ways to help.

We had to cut our church budget this year, which included cutting our salaries. My husband and I have young kids, and since our church-sponsored medical plan specializes in not paying claims, we've been pretty strapped. Their logic is that if they can avoid paying medical bills they can keep next year's premium down. Great! My son is just getting over a five-hundred-dollar case of strep throat. I don't know if the medical plan will pick up any of it.

We couldn't afford to have two of us on pastor's salaries, and I was ready for something new, but my husband wasn't. So he's still pastoring here.

We know several couples who copastor, but we're different in that we were married before seminary. When we graduated, we worked in separate churches—both half-time. That was pretty hard.

We like working together, so we were very pleased when this position opened up. We came in following a pretty troubled period, and wouldn't you know it, the church tried to keep it a secret from us. It had been in all the local papers: the pastor before our predecessor was accused of stealing eighteen hundred dollars from a senior citizens' fund. He ran it through his personal checking account. I'm not convinced that he was a thief, but he was pretty sloppy.

He was replaced with a scholar—a high church, anti-new hymnal guy. Within six months they were having secret meetings about him. Because he was a scholar, he spent a lot of time studying and preparing, so they thought he was just lazy. He fought for his job for five years. Is this a classic dysfunctional community or what?

Things were pretty touchy, but we finally found out what had been going on, so we concentrated on a healing and caring ministry. We tried to work on creating a church as the church should be. It got better after that.

We had a pretty good balance of the old guard and new people. The old guard didn't want any change; the new people wanted to experiment with everything! But the two groups were able to work together. Then, when the economy just crashed and hit bottom, the new people were the ones to pull up stakes and move somewhere else. What we were left with was the old guard. Many of them are pretty alienated and embittered about the economy, but they won't leave here. This is home. Without the counterbalance of the younger new people it got pretty difficult—especially in the congregational meetings.

This community, even before the economy crashed, was very distressed. It tends to have higher than average rates of teen pregnancy, sexual abuse, alcohol abuse and cancer. We have a pretty big drug problem. There's a fair amount of smuggling since we're a seaport.

The community is largely unchurched. According to polls, about 35 percent consider themselves Christians, and about 15 percent are in church on Sunday.

People are real people here, though. There's not that veneer that most people put on, and I find that refreshing. You can be a newcomer here for twenty years, or you can find a home and make an impact.

Surprisingly, there's a small but thriving arts community. You can go to plays, see art exhibits—a lot of cultural things you might not expect.

We're getting a bigger underclass, though. There have always been people here who were poor and would be poor forever. Folks who would cut a bit of firewood, poach some fish and game, collect mushrooms. A lot of Hispanic migrant workers came here to replant trees on the clearcuts. That's provoked a racist underground. They're paid very low wages, but with everybody out of work there's some resentment that they'll work so cheap and take jobs that locals might have gotten. This resentment complicates the pastoral ministry because it colors everything.

Timber has always been boom or bust. When the housing market slumps, timber suffers. People would be conservative, putting a bit away when things were good so that they could ride out the bad times. We've had some bad years, but things were almost back to normal when this spotted owl thing hit.

The newspaper headlines started screaming disaster, and it had a tremendous psychological effect on the whole community. Not just loggers but shopkeepers, car dealers, doctors, dentists. The pharmacist just took out a second mortgage on his home so he could stay here. He could move to the city and walk right into a high-paying job, but he's part of the community. He provides a needed service.

*   *   *

There are a lot of first- and second-generation European immigrants here. I visited a lady in the hospital and she said, "Oh, yes, I'm a member of your church." I asked her when she'd last attended. She said it was in 1942! Most people here are only marginally connected with the church, let alone with Christ.

But it's a place where it's very easy to feel at home. In a way, what happened to the rest of the country in the 1960s never happened here. People here stay put. I bury a lot of people who died in the house they were born in. That sense of continuity is unusual.

Some of the kids leave, but the ones who go to college all say they want to come back. Most of the teachers are local kids. It's not a written rule, but I doubt that they would hire a teacher who didn't grow up here. I know one guy who has a college degree, but he drives a pop truck here rather than move somewhere where he could use his degree.

I don't know what's going to happen, though. We're seeing the destruction of the middle class. The TV people talk about a new Appalachia. They want to film ragged, dirty urchins with pitiful expressions on their faces. We don't have much of that yet.

In the Reagan years there was a lot of union-busting. The truck drivers used to be union men, but now they own the trucks they drive. And now they're unemployed and have payments to make on a $100,000 truck. And nobody is buying logging trucks these days. Because they own a house and maybe a truck and a 'dozer, they don't qualify for public assistance. To qualify they have to sell everything, clean out the kids' college fund and be flat broke. It's heartbreaking.

But some of them go far away to work, even up to Alaska if they have to. They don't see their families for long periods of time, and that causes problems too.

Politicians talk about rehabilitating the displaced loggers. The whole concept of "rehabilitation" is demeaning to these folks. Their self-concept suffers horribly.

The press focuses on the outbursts, such as when a frustrated logger said in a meeting, "If we can't log the trees, we'll burn them down." He didn't mean that. These people love the forest. They work there and they play there. Yet the press portrays them as these "dumb loggers" who want to rape the environment. Loggers are very concerned with stewardship of the environment. For them, logging and working in the mills is a dignified job that provides a needed service.

They feel like the yuppies have cut the trees down in their cities and suburbs and now they want to preserve the forest so they can have someplace to play.

If people are so concerned about the global environment, they might think about where the lumber is going to come from. It will just be cut in tropical rain forests. Our climate in the Northwest is perfect for renewing forests, but the tropical rain forests don't grow back.

People here want to preserve the planet; they just don't see why their whole way of life has to be destroyed to do it. You could do much more for the environment by making people in the cities give up the private automobile. That wouldn't be nearly the hardship that closing down logging is, and it would do more environmentally.

In terms of ministry, a lot of well-meaning churches in the cities jump on the "stewardship of the earth" bandwagon without thinking about the people who are affected. It's hard for Christians out here to read about Christians who don't seem at all concerned with their very real problems.

I get pretty hot about this, because I see the loss of dignity, the harm done to families. We started our Timber Outreach to help the situation. People out here are doing what they can to make it—gathering ferns and mushrooms—but they've always done that.

Two facets of my job as pastor are to go to other churches and to talk to the media. Loggers are being vilified. They're the scapegoats.

My message is "Please do not devalue my people's pain." It's getting down to who's human and who's not. Politicians and environmentalists preface their comments by saying, "I know it's hard for the logging communities, but ..." This sends the message that some people are just not as important as other people.

Last year one of our people had some land that he was offered $2.5 million for. A developer wanted to build homes on it. He wouldn't sell, because he wanted it to be logged and replanted. He could have walked away a millionaire, but he loves the forest and he didn't want it cut down to make houses. For him, it was a question of Christian stewardship—managing the earth's resources in a responsible way. Now he can't log it, and he's a villain if he tries to explain his plight.

When I go to other churches, people tell me that they want to be stewards of the earth because the Bible tells us to. That's true, but the Bible also calls us to care for our neighbor and seek justice. If you want to go verse for verse, the passages about justice for our neighbor vastly outweigh the verses about the environment. We have to live in tension in a fallen world. We can't just say, "It's going to be like this."

My message to Christians in the city is that there are people an hour's drive away from you who are losing everything they've worked for. They're losing their dignity and self-worth! How, as Christians, do you respond to your neighbors' pain?

People also say that they want to preserve the earth for future generations. That's fine, but the communion of the saints teaches us that past, present and future generations are all important.

There's a kind of polarization that reminds me of Nazism. These people are important; these ones are not. When you polarize an issue, you have to cut off the ends.

I wish people understood that it's the little people, the workers, who are suffering. Environmentalists say that it will only hurt the big corporations. Rubbish! They'll buy land cheap, and when the pendulum swings again they'll make a killing.

Maybe if my people lose everything and become "The Poor," Christians will take notice. Maybe then they can try to minister to them when it's too late.

Another part of my ministry is to help people learn to work as a new kind of community. When the structure of the workplace is destroyed, people need to regroup.

We had a picnic where we served eleven hundred hamburgers and eight hundred hot dogs. Here are some pictures. See the woman with the T-shirt that says "Campbell's Cream of Spotted Owl Soup?" *She sighs.* I wish they wouldn't wear those shirts. It's just a joke that comes out of frustration, but it sends the wrong signal. Christian environmentalists think that these "dumb loggers" are too ignorant to understand the issues, so they don't take them seriously, or as equal brethren.

If this community really does go broke, people will have to move to the cities. Do we really want everybody to live in the city? This thing is destroying the fabric of community, which is built on honesty, hard work, reputation. In the city where I worked before this, I couldn't cash a ten-dollar check without three pieces of ID. For our picnic I cashed a twelve-hundred-dollar check by telling the cashier my phone number. People trust one another here. In the logging industry you have to trust. Guys on a log crew have to trust their lives to the fallers and the choker setters. You don't get that in the city.

A true Christian vision includes the understanding that human beings are part of the ecosystem too. Not just people individually, but people living and working together in communities. It's too easy to just say, "Oh, I'm protecting the environment." If we're really Christ's people, we have to care for the people as well as for the trees. I hate to see Christians just take a "for or against" position. All of life is complex. There are more than two sides to an issue like this. There are many, many sides.

For Christians the questions should be, What's at stake? Who wins? Who loses? How can we help those who lose? With those kinds of questions, we then have to ask prayerfully: What ought we to do? What is real stewardship in this instance? That's my pastoral role.

Seeing
Indian People
Delivered

23

The coastal Indian village is literally at the end of the road. Small frame houses line the streets of the reservation, and little fishing boats line the banks of the river. A pounding Pacific surf crashes against the sandbar at the outer edge of the lagoon.

It's a bustling place, with its own fish-processing plant, a K-12 school and a modern supermarket/café. Kids play in the street on this Saturday morning. A late autumn wind whooshes through the little town, stirring up cat's-paw ripples on the lagoon.

The power is off as I arrive at the café, which is staffed by Indian women. They are serving coffee out of air pots until the road crew can repair a line severed by a fallen Douglas fir.

I call the pastor from the pay phone to let him know I've arrived. I begin to describe myself so that he'll know me, but he cuts me off, laughing, "I won't have any trouble picking you out, Stefan." As I look around, I realize that I'm the only white man in the village.

He arrives in a few minutes and, sure enough, is able to spot me in the crowd. He's a ruggedly good-looking man with strong Indian features. He has the solid build of a man who can work in the woods or on the sea.

We take our coffee to a booth by the window. He seems to know everyone in the place by name. Kids come up to him and hug him. A little boy sits on his lap for a while and then wanders off.

*   *   *

I grew up on the reservation. I've traveled around, preaching and teaching, in Indian country all over the U.S. and Canada, but I've lived here all my life. I've been the pastor for about twenty years. We have about fifteen to twenty families right now. It goes up to as high as fifty and it drops too, but fifteen to twenty is about average. It drops a lot in the summer, when everybody is out fishing and stuff like that.

My family has been serving the Lord for five generations now. My family abandoned the Indian religion about the turn of the century. The old people have told me all about those days. I've always liked to visit the old people and talk with them. I'll tell you the story the way my grandmother told it to me.

My grandmother was chosen when she was three years old to take the Indian power and serve Tamanos. In the Indian religion there were two spirits. Tamanos was like an evil spirit. Her mother (my great-grandmother) said no, that she was to serve the good spirit, so someone who served Tamanos put a curse on my great-grandmother. Well, the curse fell on my mother's little baby brother. I'm just going to tell you the way my grandmother told me.

My grandmother was holding that baby boy, and she remembers he just bent over backward so that his head touched his heel. The evil spirit was trying to break him.

The Indians at that time lived in clans, some by the river, some along the shore, some in the woods, depending on how they got their living. Well, my great-grandmother went to get a man in another clan who had power over the evil spirit.

She got him, but he said he couldn't do it because he had backslid. He'd gone on a big drunk and no longer had the power. He came anyway, and he began to chant and pray. Here's how my grandmother describes it. She heard a song, as if it were a long way off. It came closer and closer, and then it came out of the man. To the Indians this meant that the man was in the power. While the song was coming out of him, he walked over and grabbed the evil spirit out of the baby and threw the spirit away. The baby was delivered, but that man died. He knew he was going to die, but he died for the baby.

From that day on, the Indian religion was broken in my family and they tried to live for the Lord. My grandmother said that even before they had Scripture, they had moral laws like the ones in the Bible. But later my grandmother heard the Word of God, so from that day on they followed the Lord. Now my son is married, and he and his kids follow the Lord too.

We've had our problems; I don't mean that my family has been perfect. But we've followed the Lord. Sometimes people will say that Christianity is just a white man's religion. They say, "Hey! How come you teach that white man's stuff?" But that's just a cop-out. I just ask them where they got that truck, or those tennis shoes, or that outboard motor. Indians didn't make all that stuff either.

Every village or town or city has a prince, according to Scripture. We have to rely totally on the name of the Lord, and that's what we teach in our church. We're called a cult by some of the believers in the area, because we don't teach the rapture. We believe that God has his kingdom on this earth.

We believe in prophecy. We're a Pentecostal church, and we're independent. I used to argue a lot with people over doctrine. I'd fight with people like the Jehovah's Witnesses and the Indian Shakers. One night I was doing the dishes while my wife was away, and I heard a voice. It came from the refrigerator, and it said: "I will save whom I will save, and I will condemn whom I will condemn." That startled me, and I found out later that it came from Scripture. So since then I just preach and teach, but I don't condemn people.

I found some notes I wrote back before that time. I was involved in a long-standing argument with a guy about Scripture and doctrine. I said to myself, "Oh no. Did I say that?" I went back and apologized to the guy I'd been rude to. It was eleven years later and he said he didn't remember, but I know he did.

What I like most about being a preacher is teaching the Word and seeing Indian people delivered from drugs and alcohol. That's a big problem with Indian people, and Christ can deliver you.

People can be hard to understand, though. Especially church people. How can I say it? They get stubborn and set in their own ways. Being a pastor is like being a coach. The other day at basketball practice, the girls wanted to do it their own way. But when they really learn the game and start playing the right way, then they'll start winning some games. The pastor has to be a coach and show the people how the game is played.

Some of the church people think I'm too lenient. But I used to be such a total right-winger, maybe I'm afraid of being that way again.

If a person thinks he's being called of God to be a pastor, he needs to get the simple basics down first. He needs to know the Scriptures.

When we started a Bible school here on the reservation, an old man whom I really respect said, "Let me give you some fatherly advice. Teach 95 percent grace and 5 percent law!" *He laughs.* In many schools it's just the opposite. That man is very wise. He's the one I call when I have trouble.

The people here, even the non-Christians, call me Brother Jim. I've worked alongside them over the years, and I've learned, sometimes the hard way, to follow that man's advice.

You can't be too hard on people. You have to be firm, but give the benefit of the doubt. And be willing to learn.

When I first started pastoring, Halloween came up on a church night. All the kids were excited, so I said, "Let's just cancel church and go to Halloween!"

"Yea!" they all shouted.

I studied the Word and found out later: Oops! You have to be grounded in the Word of God.

Among Indian people it's usually the women who give their hearts to the Lord first. The men come later. Maybe it's that way with white people too. I don't know.

*   *   *

There was a place in the next state called Little Chicago where Indians were getting killed every week. It was really a terrible place. We went down there, my friend and I, and held a revival. Not much happened, though.

We went again a couple of years later, and a big revival broke out. About 150 people got saved, including some big drug dealers. Some drug dealers even got saved in prison, talking to people on the telephone. Some lives were changed there.

I'm glad the Lord called me to preach. My parents were the worst alcoholics in the whole reservation. They were good people, but the bottle just had a grip on them and kept them backsliding. We kids had to pretty much raise ourselves.

I said when I was a boy, "God, if you let me become a man, I'll never put that bottle to my lips." God has blessed me, and even though we don't have the numbers of people that we'd like to have in the church, we see Indian people delivered. That's what makes it all worthwhile for me.

Maintaining
a Witness in
the Glitter

24

He's a priest to the entertainment community in Hollywood. His goal is to maintain a Christian witness among the people who produce movies and television. His priestly order works mainly with people outside the Roman Catholic Church.

His small organization offers a prestigious annual award for programming that furthers human values. He also produces television programs and movies of the week. He's now working on his second feature film. His office, in an old, Spanish-style building that was once a restaurant, looks more like a humble mission parish than the headquarters of a production company whose media projects can cost millions of dollars.

He's in a meeting when I arrive, so I wait in the reception area. His secretary, who looks like a college student, resumes her paperwork. It's quiet and peaceful. The furniture is old, the carpets are worn, but it feels remarkably homey.

The meeting ends, and the secretary ushers me into his office, where I find a relaxed, gentle, deeply intelligent man of sixty or so. He's tall and healthy-looking, with a physical vibrancy that comes in part from daily swims in the Pacific Ocean just across the highway.

*   *   *

I suppose a lot of folks think of this town as a modern Babylon or Sodom, but my experience is that there are some really fine people here too. There's a hunger for the transcendent, especially among many of the writers and actors. There's not a lot of religion in the traditional sense, because many of these people are uprooted from their backgrounds and old neighborhoods. They are definitely seekers, but they don't want a lot of God talk.

By "God talk" I mean using old clichés without really thinking about what they mean. These people are interested in what religion has to offer in the way of addressing the human condition, but most of them are uninterested in joining a respectable church. They're not churchgoers, but they are God-wrestlers.

Recently NBC asked me to host a panel for writers and directors on television's responsibility to the public. The idea was to talk about the public's need for spiritual and moral direction, and for programming that doesn't preach but allows people to think about the big questions and wrestle with them.

I know that the bosses said, "You have to be there," so a lot of the people showed up under duress, but many of them wanted to come because they're frustrated by their inability to address moral issues creatively. The whole ratings system makes it hard to do more than serve up something bland and inoffensive.

Our goals in this ministry are to evangelize the viewing audience, to maintain a gospel presence in the industry and to be a goad to the industry. We always try to remember that.

We are also a production company, and we have to follow the same rules as everyone else. We get an idea, and then I have to go pitch it to the network or studio people. I have to convince them that the program or movie will be a success and make money for them.

Whenever I work on a film or television project, I ask myself, "What's the gospel density in the show?" In other words, to what extent does it proclaim the gospel in a bold way? There are lots of movies and television shows that touch obliquely on gospel ideas of love, forgiveness, justice and so forth. We want gospel *density*. We want to preach and evangelize as strongly as possible within the constraints of commercial media. People have to buy tickets for a movie or turn the channel to your show because they *want* to see it. Can we still make a strong gospel witness?

We also think about gospel cost-effectiveness. How much moral capital is involved? Will the show motivate generosity? If you're doing a film about a famine in Africa, will it motivate people to be not only empathic but also generous? Will they get involved?

The challenge is to do this in a fresh way, without the God talk. You have to be open, interested and willing to take chances. If you just give these people the old standard lines, they'll politely ignore you. I can't be effective if I'm just "The Priest."

Everybody knows I'm a priest. I've been doing this for about twenty years. I don't like to wear clericals if I'm pitching a movie of the week to a studio executive or something like that. If the job calls for a suit and tie, then that's how I dress. If I'm trying to pitch a movie, I have to sell it on its merit. Will people watch it? Will it get good ratings? Pitching a project can be pretty intense, because you're asking network executives to put a lot of money—not to mention their reputation and career—on the line for your idea.

If I go in dressed as a priest, they may feel that they can't take the gloves off. They'll be polite and condescending. They won't ask the tough questions, and I won't get to make a strong case. It'll be "Thank you, Father. Wonderful idea. Don't call us, we'll call you." I wear clericals for funerals and things when I'm being a priest in the liturgical sense. Clericals can get in the way of communication, but people also want me to look like a priest.

When we filmed our movie in Mexico, I wore a cross when I worked on the set. Technically, priests aren't supposed to wear clericals out in public in Mexico. After the revolution in the beginning of this century, the power of the church was severely curtailed. The government didn't want the church to have any political power. In some provinces, like Tabasco, priests were hunted down and executed. Graham Greene writes about this in his novel *The Power and the Glory.* When I said mass on the set I wore priest clothes, though.

A priest is kind of a God symbol, a transcendent symbol if you will. People may be agnostic, but they do respect the idea of a "man of God." They know that I make $125 a month and that I live and work here in a building that doesn't belong to me. If they believe that I'm not out to get something for myself, they can be pretty open with me.

It doesn't matter so much to these people that I'm a Catholic, or even a Christian for that matter. I end up being priest to a lot of Jews, for instance. I've done a number of Jewish funerals, and some of the Jewish guys will talk to me about family and spiritual problems.

Most of the Jewish people here are nonobservant. Like many of the people from Christian backgrounds, they're distrustful of the clergy. Most of the Jews I work with don't like rabbis, because traditionally a rabbi will charge for a funeral. They know that I wouldn't take their money if they offered it.

It's not the money itself; they can usually afford it. It's that the rabbis—and most other clergy—aren't around. You don't see them at parties or doing seminars. So it kind of grates when you have to call them up at a time of grief and ask what a funeral will cost.

That's not to say that I don't ever ask for money. *He laughs.* When I call up they know that I might ask them for money for a project like the awards we give each year. That's an interesting situation, by the way. The church asks the industry for money, which it then uses to reward people for promoting Christian and human values. But that's what I mean about people here being God-wrestlers. They give quite freely and generously, but I don't ask them to pay *me* for services rendered. I visit the hospital or do a funeral as a friend. I pitch movies and so on as a member of their community.

Show business is like a big club. We do each other favors all the time, and in a sense chits are owed. Lew Wasserman, the head of MCA, has given over $100,000 to our work. Norman Lear, too. Lew and Norman both come from Jewish backgrounds, but they're seekers.

Fundamentalists revile these guys as anti-God, antifamily, but that's just not so. Lew Wasserman was bewildered and hurt when the pickets for *The Last Temptation of Christ* showed up at his home and portrayed him as a Christ-killing Jew. Lew's role in the production of the movie was almost nothing. He's the head of the parent corporation that owns Universal Studios.

The script for *The Last Temptation* was written by Paul Schrader, who comes from the Christian Reformed Church. He based the script on a novel written by a Greek Orthodox author. Marty Scorsese, the director, is a Catholic.

So these three guys with Christian backgrounds make a movie that angers some fundamentalists, most of whom did not see the movie, and the fundamentalists go after the Jewish executive in charge of the corporation. And they go after him in a hurtful, personally offensive way. Wasserman had almost nothing to do with the content or message of the film, yet the pickets went after him. That was cruel and shameful. You can imagine the kind of witness that sort of thing makes in the community.

Lew called me and he was deeply hurt. Not afraid for his business; deeply and personally hurt. "What's going on?" he asked. "What have I done?" I don't think those people know what it's like for a Jew of Lew's generation to be picketed and reviled as anti-Christ. It stirs up terrible memories of pogroms back in Europe. Not just the Nazis, but the regular Europeans who would attack Jews on Easter. I told him I considered that kind of behavior a countersign of the gospel.

Again, I—we—try to maintain a witness in the community. That means knowing the people and loving them. And it means liking them. You can't minister to anyone if you look down on them. You have to understand the world they live in and the constraints they live under.

You have to be humble, too. If your own house is not in order, you can't go throwing the first stone. Remember, the protests about *Last Temptation* came on the heels of the Jim Bakker and Jimmy Swaggart scandals. People in the industry saw the protests as an angry backlash by people whose leaders had disgraced them in public.

We don't have a lot of Christians who want to work with the entertainment community. There are a number of Protestant churches— Hollywood Presbyterian, for instance—that have fellowship groups for media people. Those groups are quite positive. But to be a priest to the community requires a long-term, possibly a lifelong, commitment. That's a lot easier for me because I'm celibate. I couldn't do this job if I had a wife and children, because in a sense the people here are my family. I have to be deeply involved in a lot of people's lives if I'm going to have any impact. Involved for years and years.

The church is pretty cautious when it comes to working with Hollywood. For a while I served under a bishop who was an old parish kind of guy. My "parish" is the creative and business community, and that's hard for some church officials to understand if they came from a place where your parish was a church and a school in a neighborhood with geographical boundaries.

On the other hand, I've been very free to work. I think some people assume that we have to clear everything we do with Rome, but that's not the case. The pope saw our last movie when it came out, and he liked it, which is very gratifying, but he never demanded to see the script in advance. He's been quite supportive, although he doesn't get involved in what we do here.

In the Catholic Church you are a priest for life. You can be reassigned, but you can't just get fired by an angry bunch of deacons or elders. That does allow me to take more chances, I suppose.

I remember going to an interdenominational conference with a bunch of clergymen. As we got to know each other, I was impressed at how preoccupied some of the Protestants were with being popular. They seemed to have a very strong need to be liked and approved of. I suppose that's in part because they could lose their jobs if they got a couple of people in the congregation mad at them.

On the other hand—*he laughs*—Catholic priests used to be a bit too cavalier in the days when everyone had to go to mass and confession. It was like "Hey, you have to go to mass or it's a mortal sin. I'm the priest and that's that." So if Protestants worry too much about being popular, some priests don't worry enough. Priests and ministers have to be responsive to the needs and beliefs of the people they minister to, but you can't just always give them what they want. There's a balance there, and both traditions have their strong and weak points.

But on balance, I'd have to say again that if I were married and had a family, I probably couldn't do this job. Or at least I couldn't give it what I give it now. The late nights, the traveling, the emotional commitment would make it easy to neglect a family. I was just talking to the children of a well-known Christian leader in the labor movement. She's considered a candidate for sainthood by many, but her children, who are now well into adulthood, are still very bitter about what they see as her neglect of them during their childhood.

Hollywood is a busy, hectic, demanding place. A lot of good families fall apart because of the stress and the temptations. It could be hard on anyone who works here, not just a priest.

The temptations are there, but I've never been tempted by alcohol or drugs. Not because I'm purer than others, but because it just holds no allure for me. I suppose there are people who'd like to see if I would fall, but most are supportive.

I spend time in prayer every day. That's essential for me. And I live with other priests who are quick to tell me if I'm going the wrong way. They are not the least bit impressed by whatever stature I have in the community. If I'm out of line they tell me, just as I'm supposed to tell them. I also serve in a local parish, celebrating mass and so on. If I left all that and just worked as a producer, I might be more tempted. I have to keep my anchor points.

But really, people look out for me. In Mexico when we were filming, there was a lovely girl who worked on the set. She was a delightful person whom I liked and respected, and once she gave me a big hug. One of the Mexican cameramen came up to me and said, "Hey Padre, you're a priest. You better watch it."

I laughed and said, "She's my sister in Christ. Don't worry."

He said, in a nice but firm way, "Well, that didn't look like the way you hug your sister."

I appreciated his concern and his openness. I have to remember that even though I'm the priest, I need to listen to my brothers and sisters. Even if I think they're making too much out of something.

I guess that's where my role as a priest is like any other. I live and work with the people I serve. I love them and I like them. I respect them, and I try not to come in as some condescending or arrogant moral authority.

They are very good and kind to me in return. That Mexican cameraman confronted me in love because we had a relationship and he felt responsible for my well-being.

People in this industry need to feel loved and accepted. The church spends too much time criticizing the entertainment industry. If Christians want to have a real impact, they have to show these people that they love them. If producers and directors and writers and actors feel that the church loves them—just as Christ loves them—we can ultimately have more of an impact on the quality and content of programs than if we simply confront and complain.

If our only contact with people in this industry is to coerce them, we'll just turn them away from the gospel. Like Lew Wasserman and *The Last Temptation.* He really couldn't understand why people were going after him in such a mean way.

Norman Lear, who did "All in the Family," did a few episodes of a show awhile back called "Sunday Dinner." He got a lot of flak, because people thought it was mocking God and religion. But Norman was really wrestling with some issues of faith. He said recently, "There is something genetic in the human makeup that longs for God, and people will never be satisfied until they find him." Norman's not a churchgoer yet, but he's had a spiritual rebirth.

If you're looking for people to be "born again" in the sense that they jump on board right now, you'll be pretty frustrated here. But if you see the idea of a lifelong spiritual journey, there's lots to do in Hollywood.

Sometimes the Pain Is That Close to the Surface

25

As the chaplain for the women's prison, she spends her workdays behind bars. It's her day off, and we meet for coffee in a little espresso café in a country town. We haven't met before, but I recognize her when she pulls into the parking lot.

She's a vibrant woman who looks much younger than her sixty years. She's gracious, well educated and articulate, but she's also tough and confident. We choose a table near the window and order coffee.

*   *   *

*M*y congregation is quite different from most. I know that you have substance abuse and sexual abuse in all congregations, but here *(she shows me a graph)*. Some people from the university did this, and it reflects what I already know. Ninety percent of my congregation have severe drug or alcohol abuse problems. Sixty-seven percent have been victims of significant sexual abuse. A very high percentage have tried to kill themselves. The drugs and suicide attempts are just ways to cover the pain.

This kind of ministry is more intense, and there's a lot less support. The state expects its employees to be working 100 percent of the time.

If there's a ministers' conference, I can't go unless I take vacation time. A regular priest or minister may work five and a half days, but part of that time is spent networking, sharing and relaxing.

When you work for the state, you get cut off. There's little support from your fellow clergy. My friends ask me why I left the ministry. My bishop asked me, "How do you see yourself related to the church?" What do they think I'm doing? I think of myself as a missionary, but they don't really know what I do.

My congregants are in a constant state of crisis. Most of them are in extreme stages of grief. They've been arrested, which is very stressful; they've been in jail, handcuffed, searched. They've been viewed in their entirety by people who are not their friends, but people they perceive as adversaries or enemies.

They're dealing with the loss of friends, family and self-respect. They lose all their possessions, either through theft or to the lawyers. When they get arrested, people burglarize their apartments. What little they bring into the prison often gets stolen, so they're penniless, stripped people.

The state can search their room or their person at random. It's like burglary. They also have to give urine samples on demand. That means having someone watch while you urinate, which is a hard thing for most women. They just sued the state about pat searches being done by male guards. The system is very macho, and the guards don't see why they have to go looking for a female guard every time they need to search an inmate. But if you're a woman, having a man run his hands all over you is just like being raped, just as you were raped all your life. The crisis just continues.

The inmate congregation is skewed educationally, too. Out of three hundred inmates we have two M.A.s that I know of, but most are almost illiterate. Many can scarcely read, so I have to give them a simplified Bible.

You think of people as having "pegs of knowledge" that you can hang concepts on, but these folks have fewer pegs. Many of them are mentally damaged from drugs and abuse, so they don't have much to work with. It's not at all like society at large.

There's a lot of violence in their lives. The death notices they get are horrendous! They'll get a note that says, "Your brother was sitting in the back of a truck and somebody shot him," or "Your sister overdosed." Maybe a friend died of AIDS, or a husband died in jail or prison. Then they can't go to the funeral. Funerals are important. You need to be surrounded by people who love and support one another. In prison it's just "Well, tough for you, baby!" They miss out on the most basic and important kinds of natural therapy.

So mentally, spiritually, socially, in every possible way, they are the most needy people you could ever meet. I decided a while back that I'd meet with every person who comes in here. I have a little form that asks their religious preference, the name of an emergency contact. I try to make a friendship contact. I find out how long she's going to be in here—five years, twenty years, life. Then I know how long she has to survive in here.

If she's a Christian, I give her a choice of Bibles. I try to give her a Bible she can read and understand. Of course, if she feels that the King James Version came down on a golden thread, I have to respect that. We can get lots of King James Versions—all kinds of organizations will give them away—but the simpler versions cost money and are harder to get.

Nearly 90 percent of the women who come in here check the box that asks if they'd like to talk to me. Not just the Christians, but the Muslims, Jews and Native Americans, too. I ask them how things are going. I wait, and then they start to cry. The pain is that close to the surface.

I have some pastoral care assistants—people from the community. They have no counseling skills or theological training, but they're better than nothing. They do what I'm supposed to be doing but can't because I have to do all the typing, filing and paperwork.

I run three church services each Sunday, plus a once-a-month sweat lodge for the Indians. I have to supervise religious diets for the Jewish and Muslim worshipers too. For Ramadan I have to see that they have a sack lunch for after sundown. For Hanukkah I help to find out which foods in the kitchen come from kosher cans. It's surprising how much of our food is kosher. Jewish families also bring in foods, and I helped one woman get her own special pans in the kitchen that only she could use. So much of the Jewish faith is centered around home and hearth; it's important.

If they have a chaplain who doesn't care about their special religious needs, it just increases the feeling of helplessness. They learn to manipulate when they feel helplessness, just as kids do. But that's how a lot of them got in here. They need to overcome those feelings.

We had a rabbi from the military base who used to come in. He was wonderful, but they shipped him out to the Gulf War and he didn't come back to this area. It's very hard to get "small faith" clergy, like Jehovah's Witnesses and Seventh-Day Adventists, to come in. We did have a Native American chaplain who took care of the whole prison system for the state, but he's retired now so I have to help out. I just got a braid of hair with some ribbon in the mail to give to an Indian gal. It's supposed to be a sacred item. We aren't allowed to pass on keepsakes—which is just as well, or we'd be inundated—so I have to research it to find out if it's a bona fide religious item. Many things are sacred to the Indians, but it might just be a souvenir too.

The sweat lodge has to be set up according to special principles. The fire is started at 8:00 a.m., and then special rocks that won't explode are heated. The lodge is a hut with blankets and poles, and the rocks are taken in and put in the center. They pour water over the rocks and sit in there praying. It's for purification and to get messages from Grandfather. Grandfather is God in the Native American faith.

You have to be a chaplain for all faiths. Those who can't comply shouldn't be chaplains. As a Christian I can say, "Here's what I believe and why." I can answer questions, and I feel fine about that. But not everyone can live by those rules.

In here, though, there's much more overlap. Protestants go to Catholic worship, whites go to black worship, and people of all faiths might go to a Mormon or Jehovah's Witness service.

I'm so busy just keeping everything rolling, I don't have much time to really counsel or disciple. Office work is nearly 100 percent of my job. Have you ever been in a job where you have to document everything that you do in a day? The state doesn't really have an idea in the world what I do.

There's so much repetitive work like typing, filing, answering the phone, writing a simple thank-you letter. I'm about to petition the state to give me a full-time secretary to help me with it.

A young woman, an inmate, came bounding into my office the other day and told me that she heard I needed an assistant. She wanted the job. She'd been a chaplain's assistant in the military, she is a Christian, she knows how to do the job and she likes to share her faith. But . . . inmates can't use the phone. We have a confidential code for phoning outside the prison, and I can't give it to a prisoner. They can't write on prison stationery; they can't have access to names and addresses. And they can't even be in the office unless I'm there. So it's hopeless.

Volunteers don't work out either. After a while they decide that they should be getting paid. And most volunteers also decide they'd rather preach. They don't come when they say they will, so I'm stuck with a huge backlog. No, I need a full-time, paid secretary with the skills to do the job.

We're getting more and more inmates, which means more turnover and less time for me to do my job.

Inside each one of these hardened criminals is a sweet little girl who's built up a tough image to survive. She needs a big mouth and attitude to live on the street. I'd get murdered if I tried to live on the street. I'm not tough enough. I'm just not streetwise. She has to be able to get in a stranger's car, perform sexually, get the money and live through the evening.

One mother, a drug addict, came in to talk. She told me her story, the abusive childhood, the whole story. She said, "I swore I'd never . . ." Then the tears. She didn't know how to stop the pattern.

We have about twelve women who are in for life without parole. They expect to die in prison. I wonder if maybe death is kinder. One came in when she was twenty. *She shakes her head, fights back tears.* That's just cruel.

It costs about one million dollars to keep a person in prison for life.

Women are more expensive than men because they have more health problems: pregnancy, abortion and so forth. They come in pregnant, or they get pregnant at a work camp. They're starved for affection and male contact. They go behind a bush and get pregnant.

If they want an abortion, they have to talk to the prison doctor and me. I am supposed to be nondirective. I ask them if they've had other children, other abortions. I ask, "Does that seem okay?" I ask them if they've thought about the moral and spiritual implications of the pregnancy.

One young woman told me she didn't know what God wanted. We talked, and the next day she was beaming. She said, "God wouldn't want an abortion!"

I've seen the products of the unwanted or crisis pregnancies. It's not a pretty sight. But I've never, and I mean never, met an inmate who would ever consider adoption! They'll abort, but they won't put their babies up for adoption. I'm not sure why that is, but it probably has to do with their own sense of not belonging, of being abandoned.

One gal came in and said, "I want an abortion. I don't want to know anything about it. I just want an abortion." Those are the ones I worry about.

These gals anniversarize. Their grandfather died a year ago, and here comes the day. It might be a child, or someone they've killed. When the time approaches, they change in behavior. Some get psychotic or depressed. They cry. Sometimes they talk to me, but not to their friends. If they tell a friend, then that person is not their friend for long because it's all over the prison. Maybe it has to do with the need for marking the passage of time, but I wonder how they handle abortions, especially if they don't think about it first.

There's a lot of persecution in here. The lowest are "baby rapers" and child killers. They can't belong or have friends. On Christmas someone will hang a Baby Jesus on their door with a note that says "Merry Christmas Baby Raper!"

I don't have anybody that I talk to about my spiritual needs. I took a personality inventory once that said that I'm very cerebral. I can cry with a person, then turn right around and laugh with someone else.

I care deeply, but I don't carry it around with me. I can't. This isn't a normal life. I'm not married, and I have no kids. I live on a peaceful acreage where I garden and do quiet things. My life outside is nothing like my life inside. I couldn't survive in this job if I had a husband and kids. The job is my whole life.

We prison chaplains get together twice a year. I value that time, because although we don't talk that much, we share the knowledge of the job. We don't have to talk. We can just walk the beach and communicate nonverbally.

I get a lot of support from inmates. They'll pray for me when they know I'm down.

This is the hardest job I know of. I have to support the institution, because I'm a state employee. I have to let the institution know that I'm not running an undercover advocacy. But I have to be closer to the inmates. It's an adversarial system, "them" versus "us," and the women have to know I'm on their side.

Volunteers and friends pray for me. Without their prayers I couldn't survive.

Our former chaplain was a black man. The services were black services, and a lot of people were left out. There's no such thing as a "nondenominational" service. If you have a white service, the blacks say, "That's not for me"; if you have a Pentecostal service, the Catholics feel out of place. You have to try to meet the needs of all worship styles.

When I got here, I called a big, white, rich church and asked for help. They had an interim pastor who'd been in prison ministries, so they got heavily involved. Their choir and bell choir come regularly. They run craft projects—yes, I'm also in charge of crafts *(she laughs heartily)*—like making crosses for Africa and needlepoints for Children's Hospital. That church supplies the materials.

The best help I get is from Kairos. It's the prison version of Cursillo. Cursillo is a lay organization; it started in the Roman Catholic Church, but it's interdenominational now. *Cursillo* means "short course" in Spanish. *Kairos* is a Latin word for God. They do a three-and-a-half-day weekend where they teach the basics of Christianity.

They explain the idea of a Christian community, and they let the inmates experience full-blown Christian love. They help them to give up their unforgiveness—of the father who raped them, the mother who wasn't there, any unforgiveness that is hampering them in their becoming fully Christian. We've had a lot of deliverances happen at those weekends as a result of felt love. Those are the most supportive folks. They give the inmates a short course on God.

One woman was a four-time loser, a real hard-core heroin addict. She's been clean for two years now and has a job. She told me, "I found in Kairos and Jesus what I looked for in heroin all those years!"

We have over two hundred volunteers—black, white, Hispanic, Pentecostal, Catholic, Lutheran, Adventist, Mormon, you name it. There are no nondenominational services. Every service has its roots in some kind of denomination.

I did do a kind of nondenominational service at Thanksgiving, though. I had people write on a 3x5 card what they were thankful for. If I let them speak up, some just mumble, while others take up the whole service. Anyway, a black gal led us in some African-American hymns, and then I read a few cards. Then a white gal led us in some songs, and I read a few more. They really loved that service, but really they need more discipling than that.

Seasonal times are really hard for them. For a normal congregation, seasonal holidays are times of great joy. I never saw anything end so fast as Christmas in prison. By 9:00 a.m. Christmas morning, all the decorations were down and it was a thing of the past. It was just too hard. But now they're pestering me for Christmas cards, and it's barely December. They anticipate far in advance, but when it comes they can't wait to end it. I guess it's just too painful for them.

I cry for them at Christmas. We had a party for moms and their kids. When it was over, I was in the visitors' room and saw the social workers taking the kids away. Kids were screaming in panic as they were pulled out of their mothers' arms. *Again, she fights tears.* It's just so tragic.

They need to be fixed on the inside for things to change. There's nothing on the outside that will make one bit of real difference. The director of prisons said a while ago that there are two things that are most influential in keeping inmates from reoffending and coming back: family ties and religious conversion. I don't know if he's a Christian, but that's what he said.

Yet they act as though religion were the least important thing in the world. It's odd. It's a macho system that doesn't go in for love. The officers—a majority anyway—just say that the inmates are hypocrites when they get religion. They say that they're just trying to impress the judge. Well, in First Corinthians it says that love hopes and endures. There's got to be somebody within the system who believes in them!

I get so mad when I hear someone say, "Why would anyone want to marry an inmate?" They forget that inmates are human beings with all the same hopes and dreams as anyone else. It's like the slave owners, who justified their cruelty by saying, "Sure we have to break up the family, but it doesn't hurt these people like it would us." Rubbish.

I suppose some officers feel they have to be that way to do their jobs. If you saw the inmates as people, it would be hard to be an officer, I suppose. There are a few shining examples—officers who listen to inmates and respect them—but they're the minority.

Many inmates have said to me, "I'm so glad I came to prison because otherwise I wouldn't have met Jesus." *She tears up again.* A wonderful old lady who'll die here told me that not too long ago. Others say, "If I hadn't come to prison I'd be dead from the drugs, or murdered."

We do a good job of offering them their faith in a way they can understand and accept it, but when they get out they're like a little plant in a hostile environment. Nobody pays any attention to them.

Everybody wants to preach to inmates and put a little notch on their belt. But inmates can hear that seven days a week. What folks don't realize is that if inmates only hear about conversion, they'll think that that's the whole story. They need to be discipled, inside and outside of prison. They need people who'll pick them up and take them to lunch, or phone them and ask how they're doing.

There was a little addict who came in here all with her arms all abscessed from injecting the drugs, but when she got clean she was a beautiful girl. When she got out, she had a job at an insurance agency. She looked just lovely. She lasted till noon. Then she went out and got high. She came back in here a while later looking like a little slut, with a wig hanging off her head.

What happened? She knew that her fellow workers all knew who she was and where she was from. She knew that they didn't want to know her. She needed a friend, so she called an old one, and that old "friend" said, "Let's get high."

They don't have friends on the outside. They call and write me, but I'm swamped. My dream is a network of people who'll welcome inmates back into town. I need people I can call and say, "Will you take care of her?" Someone who would take her to lunch, or shopping. Not spend money, or take her into their house, just welcome her and be a spiritual friend.

I've never seen it happen, though. People don't see that kind of help as romantic. They like to preach to a captive audience and then swagger around telling people, "Praise God, there were four souls saved today!" But who wants to go shopping with a jailbird?

Some folks want to start a halfway house. But those things often become big productions that eventually fold. Inmates just need personal friends.

I wouldn't send a full-blown sociopath out to someone, just a sister who needed a hand up. It's like when I lived in Alaska for a while. I spent a long time out in the bush, and when I returned to Fairbanks I was almost intimidated by the running water. Not just cold, but hot too! I was afraid to cross the street.

A man got out of prison and needed razor blades. He went to a store and saw all this stuff! It hurt to just stand there, but he didn't want to ask for help or they'd know where he'd been. In prison, a guard handed him a razor and then took it back when he was finished. In the store there are Bic and Gillette, disposable, twin-blade. He began to tremble because he didn't know what to do.

They need somebody to take them to church. They want to go, but they're afraid to go by themselves. If they walk in with Mr. and Mrs.

So-and-So, they figure people will accept them. They need someone to take them to AA meetings the first time or two.

That's where the whole system breaks down. I've never seen it come together. Now we're getting Mexican migrants who've smuggled drugs. They have no family, because they're all in Mexico. I ask for a phone number, but there's no phone. These folks are just lost when they get back out.

A lot of inmates have been disowned by their families. Sometimes for good reason. Often the family is just worn-out. A lot of times they'll eventually take them back, but not until they know there's going to be a change.

A street kid had been on the streets since her early teens and had a real attitude. She was making it and didn't need any help. She had a little chin on her. Real attitude. I said, "You're pretty tough, aren't you?" She said yes. I said, "Do you ever cry?" She said no, and then the tears began to flow.

Sometimes I'll just hold them if I feel it's okay and wanted. It's totally against the rules to touch an inmate like that, but I defy anyone to tell me that I can't.

It's partly because of all the homosexuality in prison. I don't know how long the prison can keep up its rules on homosexuality, with all the agitation on the outside. Maybe there are good homosexual relationships, but in prison they are pretty sick. It causes fights and a lot of guilt. Usually it's someone who's been a victim all her life agreeing to be the lover of someone who will dominate her. It perpetuates the victim-victimizer relationship that got her in here in the first place.

I don't preach about it. I don't care if they sit together in church. I don't even care if they came to church just to be together—and they do. But if they are behaving in a way that would be unacceptable even on the outside, I'll ask them to stop.

If someone has something bad, it's better to give them something good to replace it. I don't try to just take away their relationships. But a sick or victimizing relationship will drop away when the inmate is spiritually healed.

*　　*　　*

I knew what I was getting into when I took this job six years ago. I had worked in the prison as a counselor/social worker for several years before. This job is my whole life. It's where my heart is.

A prison chaplain needs to be in the job for a long time to build trust. Not just with individuals, but with the population. It's the inmate code. They'll say, "What about the chaplain?" If you are trusted over the years, the inmates will know it.

We had a series of one- and two-year chaplains before me. That's not a good situation. They were all men. I'm the first woman ever.

A lot of these women are man-starved. They only know how to relate to men sexually, and it gets in the way. They can tell me in gross detail all about their lives, and they know that I understand. I'm a woman, so I'm not the enemy.

One woman told me in graphic detail about being sexually abused all through her childhood. It had affected every area of her life. Just ruined her. She shook violently when she told me about it. Talking about those things helps, and I know she wouldn't have told a man. I was the first one she'd ever told. She knew, too, that I wouldn't write it down someplace so she'd be further humiliated.

You have to have a tender heart to do this job. But you can't afford to get burned out. An inmate must be really free to tell you things. Even though you've heard it all before, you have to hear each person with fresh ears. You can't let it get routine.

This is why I resent having to do all the office work while the volunteers do my job. I need time to really help people. Instead, I'm in the office doing bureaucratic stuff.

I counseled a girl on my sixtieth birthday. She was thinking about having an abortion. We prayed for the child. She decided to keep the baby. She'll remember that prayer, too. They remember things you said or prayed about when they were in crisis—even when you forget yourself. Often someone will say, "You helped me so much when you said this or that," and I won't even remember.

Inmates have to go to a job or to school. They don't just sit in their cells like everyone thinks. If they don't, they lose good time, which can reduce up to one-third of their sentence. They do all kinds of jobs—janitorial, kitchen, drafting, sewing.

At this point she pulls out some blueprints she has been working on and spreads them across the table.

I took some architecture classes in the university, so I've been drawing up the plans for a new chapel. I have a window of opportunity to get a chapel built when they add on a new section to the prison. Once they get the wing built and fill it up with inmates, they'll never let a construction crew in. But if I can get the chapel built while they're building the new wing, I can do it.

I figure it'll cost about sixty thousand dollars to put up, with volunteer labor.

She bends over the table to show me the floor plan.

See, the whole thing has windows inside, so that inmates can be together for prayer and peer counseling. The guards can watch them, but they have a bit of privacy. This is a soundproof wall between two worship rooms. That way, the black Pentecostals can worship at the same time as the Catholics without being told to keep it down. People have to be able to worship freely.

This room is a meditation chapel. It has windows too. Some inmates just need to get away from all the cussing and bickering for some quiet time. Also, smaller groups, like Muslims and Jehovah's Witnesses, could use the meditation chapel for worship services.

I've got a few years left, and then I'll retire. Before I go, I want to get a building set up so that my successor can run a program if she wants to. Right now it's not humanly possible to minister to the inmates.

If they ever give me a secretary, I could be a chaplain instead of a paper shuffler. That's my dream, anyway.

The Sixty-seventh Book

26

He came to the United States from a predominantly Muslim country in Africa,
a tortured nation that has suffered the tribulations of war, famine and disease.
A young father, with hopes of more schooling, he works in a semiskilled job and
serves as a deacon in an expatriate African church.

We meet at his place of work, during his lunch break. He's a warm, outgoing
man with a bright smile. He greets me by raising both palms, in the custom
of his homeland. When I ask how he's doing, he replies, "Fine, praise God," but
it's not pretentious. I get the feeling that he really does praise God for just about
everything good (or not bad) that happens.

*   *   *

*M*y background is Orthodox, but I didn't know Christ then. I
just went to church and prayed and tried to be a good boy.
When I was twelve, I had to leave my home in the country and go
to the capital to find work. My friend gave me a Bible in my own
language, but when I left home I gave it to my father. In the capital
I went to a Coptic church every day, but I didn't understand much.

One day I went to a Mennonite bookshop to buy a Bible. The
cashier asked me if I had received Christ as my Savior. I didn't understand the question, because I was just a country boy without much
education. She asked me, "Would you like to meet Jesus?"

I said yes! She told me to wait, and she went in the back room. I thought she was going to bring for me Jesus. *He laughs heartily.* I didn't understand why she came back with a book instead of Jesus, but I bought the Bible and began to read it.

Then one day I saw a place with a cross on the door, so I went there and met a deacon who invited me in. It was a very different kind of church, not too fancy, and people were giving testimonies. They asked me if I want to accept Jesus. I said yes. They asked me, "Are you a sinner?" I said no. *He laughs.* I was very young. But after three weeks I understood. My knees were shaking, and I asked them to help me. They put their hands on my shoulders, and I cried tears. I became a born-again Christian. God pulled me out from hell, and now I was not a devil or evil-spirit server any more.

I was working in a carpentry shop, and a missionary asked me if I would teach deaf people. I learned American Sign Language and taught the Bible to deaf people. Some of them became born-again Christians.

I was dreaming about going to school, but the school was very far away and I had no money. The missionary said, "We'll start a school." So when I was eighteen I started attending a Baptist Bible school. I studied there for three years.

Our church grew. I made the pews for the church with my hands.

Most of the people were Muslim. You can't just tell a Muslim, "Muhammad is not a prophet." You have to be friendly and go slow. Very slow. Some Muslims came to Jesus, but it took a long time. Many of my friends were Muslim.

Then I became a pastor and served for about eight years. It's not easy to be a pastor. It's hard work and a lot of responsibility. Your life must be like a mirror.

I have a saying that there are sixty-six books in the Bible, but really there are sixty-seven. Number 67 is your life. You can give someone a Bible, but the first Bible they will read is the sixty-seventh book. If they believe that one, they will read the other books.

Many times someone would come to the church and accept the Lord. They would say, "That person's life invited me." Jesus told us to be light and salt. That's very important.

I was happiest when souls were being saved and saddest when souls weren't being saved. But it was hard to do a pastor's job. Just think, in a big church you might have five hundred people. If you spent time, really good time, with a different person every day, after a year you would have met with 365 people. And only once. They would all be saying, "The pastor doesn't care about me. We had such a fine time talking and praying and reading the Word, but he never called again." And the other 135 that you never got to, they would be very hurt or mad.

But you can't spend a lot of time with everyone, because you have to spend time preaching and preparing classes and training elders. If you get asked, you might have to go to another church to preach. Also, you need to talk to the missionaries and the other pastors and your other friends. If you do all of this, you can't have time to pray for yourself. A pastor has to pray for himself, or he won't be any good to the church.

People always ask the pastor, "Pray for this, pray for that." If he prays for everything, he won't have time to pray for himself, and he won't know the Lord's will.

So I learned to pray for myself and tried to disciple others so that they could disciple others. Remember, Jesus had just twelve disciples.

The church grew and people came to know the Lord, but a couple of years later the revolution came, and it was very bad for everyone. The girls in the choir were taken to prison and treated very badly. The missionaries were evacuated from the country, and the church went underground. The government took over the church property and cut the cross from the building. That's when I became an underground pastor. I would go from house to house to teach and preach. We had to have no more than five people in each house or the government would find out and persecute us.

The government was communist, but it persecuted Christians more than the Muslims had. If they knew you were a Christian, they put you in jail and beat you. They would demand, "Do you promise you won't serve the Lord?" If you said you would keep on serving the

Lord, they would beat you some more.

Some jailers were better than others. Some jailers would let your family visit and bring food, but others would not even let the believers talk to anyone. Finally they knew I was a pastor and I couldn't go to house churches anymore. They would just follow me and arrest the whole church. I caused trouble for others, so I escaped to another country and then I came here.

Now I'm a deacon, and I'm married to a woman from my country. I met her in this country, so we were able to start out together serving the Lord and teaching our children to serve the Lord.

In my country the government would punish you for serving the Lord. Here you can serve the Lord and no one will punish you.

Part 8

Keeping the Faith

The Only Church in Town

27

He's an easygoing, instantly likable fellow in jeans and a sweater—educated and intelligent without being effete. He has worked as a carpenter, but he could be at home with businesspeople too. He speaks in a quiet, measured voice and has a soft, self-effacing smile.

We meet in the little office that is adjacent to the century-old white church. The two buildings look oddly mismatched: New England clapboard and spire next to utilitarian block. He's been working on this week's sermon, and he's ready for a break.

*　　*　　*

*T*his community has pretty traditional expectations for the pastor: preaching, counseling, visiting. I found, when I arrived here a year and a half ago, a hunger for teaching. We started a men's Bible study with ten or twelve guys, and it's still going. The women's Bible study is going well, too.

I do a lot of marital and premarital counseling. Also, a lot of people come from off-island to get married in the old church in the center of the island. I don't know if you've seen it. It's a beautiful example of a turn-of-the-century country church. It sits in a knoll amid forest and pasture. It has the little old pioneer graveyard next to it. Catholic and Protestant denominations use it for services, but the pastors are part-time or from off the island. Since I'm the only full-time pastor, I get to do a lot of weddings.

This place seems rather idyllic, but for me there is very little off time. Since the parsonage is right next to the church, and very visible, I'm on display anytime I split wood or mow the lawn. A lot of people wave, although I have no idea who they are. Sometimes I feel a bit stranded. No, that's not the right word. Everybody knows me better than I know them.

People in the church seem to be aware of this, so they don't drop by the house too much. But when I'm in the office, a lot of them will stop by.

We have a couple who work with young people. We only have four or five teenagers on Sunday, but about twenty turned out for a Josh McDowell film series. I'd like to have more facilities for them, because there's nothing to do on this island.

* * *

I enjoy meeting people who want to be fed. The islanders are open and gracious. It's a real change of pace from the city I used to pastor in.

For the first few months I felt a great need to get off the island, but now I get off only about once a month. I don't know why that is.

There's a good corps of men on the elder board. They give me background on situations and families, so I'm not completely in the dark. Some have been here for a long time; others came more recently but have good church experience.

The church was built at the turn of the century and was part of the Congregational Church and then the United Church of Christ. It struggled for many years with no pastor, and then a retired missionary from a Bible school came and helped make the transition to an independent church. He worked out a statement of doctrine.

People in this congregation come from a variety of backgrounds. In my city church, the people came because they wanted that particular type of doctrine and worship style. In this church we have everyone from charismatic to Lutheran and everything in between. Here we are *the* church, so as pastor I have to respect everyone's needs while still remaining true to my doctrinal beliefs.

The diversity in this church came through to me early. One of the older men came into the office—barged in, actually—and blurted out, "Are you opposed to Masonry?" I said, "No, of course not." I thought he said *missionaries.* When I realized we were talking about Masonry, I had to backtrack. Anyway, he said the Masons were having their once-a-year dinner, several pillars of the church were Masons, and I ought to come. It was kind of a veiled threat. I talked to the elders and decided that I shouldn't go. Back in my city church, it would have been no big deal. Nobody would have even known. Here it would be seen as a statement in support of Masonry, so I think it was good not to go.

The people here tend to be in construction, logging, fishing; there's one schoolteacher. So I guess you'd call it a blue-collar congregation. We're more or less homogeneous socioeconomically, but very diverse in terms of doctrine and tradition.

Charismatics tend to feel restricted by our worship style. We had one couple who came from a very charismatic church where they spoke in tongues and received words of knowledge. They told me they liked the teaching but felt they were too restrained in the worship experience, which tends to be pretty traditional. They said—*he laughs*—they could just as well take one of my tapes home and forgo coming to the service. They haven't been back.

Then we have some older folks—a lot of our members are retired—who don't like the new songs. They feel uncomfortable with anything that breaks with tradition.

I try to give a lot of freedom and respect everyone's backgrounds, so my focus is on our relationship with Christ. I've been preaching a long series on Mark's Gospel, and I'm going to begin a series on the church—where the resurrection left off.

We have about a hundred attending each Sunday. We had 140 on Easter and sometimes get 130 in the summer.

As the only pastor, I get a lot of opportunities to minister to the community. We have the baccalaureate service at the high school. A while back we did a memorial service with five hundred in attendance. That's almost one-third of the island.

In some ways, being the only church, and right downtown, so to speak, we're like a lighthouse. When people want a pastor or a religious service, they think first of us.

There are lots of people on the island who profess to be Christian but don't want anything to do with the church. This area is known for being "unchurched" in that sense. People tend to be pretty individualistic.

One example of my being very visible is in the way I raise my kids. My boys are eight and six. The older one has struggled in school and may have an attention-deficit disorder. He was having a lot of trouble at school—getting into fights, falling behind in his work. We pulled him out and are home-schooling him.

The last pastor took a lot of flak for doing that with his kids. Everything I do is seen as a statement, so I have to be sensitive about doing this. I don't want home-schooling to be interpreted as elitism, but I also have a responsibility to do what's best for my children. I can't make them bear the burden of my image in the community.

I wish there were another alternative. I have wondered if there is anything the church can do in the way of a school. It would be an awfully small school, though.

I am aware of how anything I do can affect my future. A job like this is not too secure. I report directly to the board. They hired me and they can fire me. It's not a good job for an insecure person.

I learned in a previous position that my identity can't be based on my job. It has to be on who I am and what I'm doing in that job.

The principles of being a pastor apply everywhere. I guess a young pastor coming into a congregation like this one should be careful not to come charging in trying to change things. Be patient. Love people where they're at. I think that these people would like me to visit more, but I'm more geared to being in my study, getting my sermons and Bible study lessons ready.

When I came they asked me, "Do you mind if you're always the pastor?" They tend to expect the pastor to take charge of everything. After the Easter service we had coffee and refreshments in the hall. I got held up for a while, and when I arrived they hadn't started eating. They were waiting for me to pray.

They look for the pastor to call the shots on everything. Even my own family does that. I went to my parents' house for Thanksgiving, and they assumed that since I was a pastor I would ask the blessing.

I don't have close men friends. There's a point where I get close, and then it doesn't get closer. I'd like to be one of the guys with these men. I hope it happens someday.

I have two good friends from Bible school; one lives on the other side of the state, the other on a nearby island. We talk on the phone, and a man in the church who works on both islands acts as a courier for us, taking books and magazines back and forth. That's really helpful.

An old school friend became a cop. He called me and we got together. It was good to just talk and laugh, without being the pastor.

One deacon, the chairman of the board, has been getting closer to me since his wife died. We talk more. I thought maybe it was a counseling thing, but it's more than that. I appreciate my times with him. I want to be here as a brother to these men, not just their pastor.

Christ
Is in History,
and So Is
the Church

28

He's a gray-haired priest in his sixties whose parish covers several islands. He's lean and fit, with bright eyes that reveal a sharp, inquisitive mind.

The Catholic community is very sparse in this part of the country, so he does a great deal of traveling by car and ferry. We meet for coffee in a little restaurant on one of the islands. In the adjoining bar a rowdy group of fishermen and loggers are watching a football game on television.

He's a remarkably personable man, easy to talk to and easy to like. We get acquainted and then begin talking about the life of a parish priest.

*   *   *

*N*o generalization is true, not even this one. People are unique, and you have to expect anything you could ever imagine. Sometimes you don't meet people's expectations, because most people have their minds made up about spiritual things. That's especially true of people with a narrow or strict set of beliefs, the ones who go on "blind faith."

Actually, the term *blind faith* appears nowhere in Scripture. But way back in the Middle Ages a break was suggested between intelligence and faith, as though you could separate them.

My dad was a trial lawyer. He taught me to question everything and to ask why I believed what I believed. In school the sisters operated more on the level of blind faith and obedience, so I had a head-on collision with them on matters of religion. They were good Christians, but we clashed.

Some people have very clear ideas about right and wrong, so they also have very clear ideas about what you should and should not be teaching: "This has value; this does not." Usually, and I don't mean this to sound as critical as it sounds, they haven't studied. Everything has value, and we always rank things according to value: 1, 2, 3, 4.

Religious belief is more will than intellect. Sometimes people can be very hurtful, especially to children, when they expect blind faith on every matter.

Kids accept faith beautifully. They should be encouraged to ask questions as they grow in their faith. The Socratic idea, to question everything as though there were no fixed values, is a pagan concept, but to question in the expectation of getting closer to the truth is a Christian concept. That's really the prophetic tradition. All through the Bible, the prophets were asking the big questions.

My dad used to say that you ought to be able to explain your ideas even when no one will listen. You need to be able to explain your ideas at least to yourself.

Some questioning—like the Clarence Thomas hearings that were so divisive a while back—is hostile. That kind of questioning is meant to be destructive. People on both sides were trying to poke holes, tear down and win. But questioning can be constructive.

Some of my dad's law partners were atheists, and these guys were trial lawyers, not corporate lawyers. They questioned me about everything, not to tear me down, but just to be questioning. So I saw questioning as a natural, good thing.

As a kid I was traumatized when some of my religious teachers didn't know how to deal with my questions. There are some priests who don't really like to deal with the big questions. I'm not saying that they're not good people, or that they're not serious Christians, but they just don't want to deal with questions. Working with these people can be pretty stressful. It's stressful because you see the harm they are doing to others around them.

When people get too convinced that they have all the answers, they can't listen to another person. They can't be with another person. I get really concerned when I see some of these TV preachers who have all the answers. They say this is good, this is bad. Period. Then people who have blindly followed them see them fall, and they have to wonder if the faith is untrue. There's no sense of incremental growth—the spiritual journey.

Some people in my parish were scandalized by Andrew Greeley's novels. How could a celibate Catholic priest write these steamy novels about sex? I read one of his novels, and I came away feeling that he was doing a good thing. Sex is the big thing that leads Americans away from the faith. It's not a bunch of screwy ideas like Marxism that challenge the American church; it's just sex. Sex is like a god, an end-all. So Greeley decided to deal with it.

I used to read Greeley's essays in the Catholic press. He's really a sharp mind, one of the brightest people we have. His essays were wonderful. They challenged and prodded, but he got so much flak from his critics, I think he must have just decided it wasn't worth it. Maybe that's why he turned to novels. He just tells his stories and puts them out there in the mainstream. It's a shame that the Catholic press didn't encourage him to deal with the tough questions.

I worry about anti-intellectual religion. St. Peter said to always be ready to *give* an answer, yet so many people just want to *have* the answer.

In about 1100, St. Abelard taught that it was good to question. That was really the beginning of the university. Questioning what life is about. He studied physical science because he knew that kind of knowledge would lead him closer to God. Until St. Abelard, the church just had monastic grammar schools. But the university in Paris was a direct result of Abelard. Later, Oxford and Cambridge came out of Paris. And the American universities came out of Oxford and Cambridge.

The more I study theology, the more I'm drawn to history, and vice versa. History and theology converge. The more you know about history, the less you can follow blind faith.

You know, it's interesting that General Rommel would not allow discussion of philosophy or politics in his officer corps. He didn't want his men thinking about those things. He knew that thinking and questioning would not result in the kind of blind obedience that he required . . . although he did forbid his son to join the SS, so he must have been thinking about something.

Sincerity is the big virtue in the U.S. There's a sense that if you're sincere, you don't have to really wrestle with the big questions. American religion is like this. We're not a society that thinks as much about the big ideas, in the Catholic colleges or in any college for that matter. People come out of college prepared to make money, but I don't get the sense that they're really educated. We used to think we needed the Catholic colleges so that the church would have somewhere to do its thinking. Now they're becoming places that prepare kids to make money.

I've been in this parish just over a year. You meet people you feel are on the same wavelength as yourself, but it takes a while to get to know them. Since this parish is so spread out, I don't get the chance to get to know people easily. Each parish is as unique as a person's fingerprint, and it takes a while to get to know it.

As a priest, you can get too caught up in the parish and let it become your whole world. When that happens you're not as effective. That's why we go on spiritual retreats.

Retreats are spiritually refreshing, but they can be exhausting. In my order we have a tradition of silent retreats. We take a thirty-day retreat when we enter the order and another thirty-day retreat when we finish our training. We also take one eight-day retreat each year. After a couple of days with no TV, no radio, no talk, you get a heightened focus and awareness.

Everybody thinks it's a vacation, but it's exhausting. It's a time for discerning the spirits. St. Ignatius of Loyola wrote rules for discerning spirits. He said that desolation, the feeling that God is far away, is okay. Good people go through these periods of dryness, but faith is persevering even when we feel numb. St. John of the Cross called this "the dark night of the soul."

Consolation is the opposite of desolation. It's when there is nothing more fun than religion. It's like at Christmas or Easter, when God seems so real and close that you can touch him. But nobody can live in a state of consolation all the time. We'd have to be sinless. When people try to artificially create a state of consolation, they either get into a sort of artificial emotionalism or they become grim and legalistic. Both are attempts to attain that state of consolation.

The Puritans were a bit like that. You know, they opposed bear-baiting not because it was cruel to the bear, but because people were having too much fun, getting too excited over a nonspiritual activity.

*   *   *

Throughout history, the clergy have been responsible for misinterpreting the teachings of Christ and getting people off the track. In today's society, the clergy are not automatically awarded the authority that they once were. That's just a reflection of our society. The concept of democracy—that each person decides what is right—is constantly broadening in North America.

The ancients taught that democracy leads to selfish people, people who want everything to revolve around their desires. That's not necessarily worse than other states, though. When the Germans were divided into little states, everybody learned to follow orders and not question authority. That's why they say that although the Bavarians are some of the most wonderful people in the world, when you give one of them a postman's hat he turns into Hitler. *He laughs.*

The Germans, with no natural frontier barriers, were always fighting wars. Dad was away a lot, and when he came home he spoke to his kids like a top sergeant. Sociologists say that the German father got along okay with his daughters, but his sons needed to leave home as early in life as possible. Dad's word was the ultimate authority. There was no room for questioning.

The Italians aren't quite like that. If Italians get together for Christmas, the son might end up arguing with his father, but they still love and respect one another.

So when those German and Irish people came to America as immigrants, they looked to others to explain things and tell them what to do. As they became more Americanized, they wanted to choose for themselves. So historically, it's more complicated than just ecclesiastical authority. It's also tied up in the ways that different societies develop.

In this time and place the clergy need to persuade people. I'm not unhappy or uncomfortable with this. It's just the time we live in. We have to remember that Christ is in history. He's alive and part of history. So we shouldn't try to freeze history.

Even in America we go into a dictatorship when we're at war. The government says what we'll do, and we all follow. If you get a bunch of Catholic marines, they might expect their priest to advise them on moral and ethical matters while they're on the base, but you get them off the base and it's a different story. Then they're subject to their field commanders, their comrades, their own free will in the particular situation. There's no one final authority for them.

Contrary to what people will try to tell you, there was never a stable period in history. In the Middle Ages you might have lived in fear that there were Huns in the forest. Theology and the way people relate to it are always influenced by the flow of history. Things are always changing, and the clergy should minister to people in the change. We shouldn't try to make things stop changing.

The idea that Christianity can be put into a concrete set of axioms is really Platonic. Plato used a geometric model to look at the universe. That's really how we get catechisms, which are axiomatic. When we try to make sense of the world, or of the gospel, independent of the development or flow of history, we can't make sense of the answer. We don't get to see the working of the Holy Spirit.

I worry about people who say, "I have the faith." We grow and develop in our faith. I used to get into quite a taffee pull with the sisters over this. My dad said that you have no right to your own opinion. It has to be based on evidence. You have to be able to explain it to the best of your ability.

It Was
a Surprise
for Us All

29

She is a lively blond woman in her thirties, with a hearty laugh and a firm handshake. We hit it off right away, as, I suspect, do others who meet her.

She is the sole pastor of an established church in a semirural, rather conservative community. This is somewhat unusual in her mainline denomination, which tends to appoint women clergy to associate ministries within large congregations. The church is housed in a traditional brick building dating to 1915, with ivy-covered walls and belfry. We meet in the pastor's study, a garreted room behind the sanctuary.

*   *   *

Well, I didn't have to fight to get this job. When I interviewed, I was an assistant pastor at a big church in a big city, where I "ran a program." The search committee wanted a man in his forties with a nurse/teacher wife and kids in junior high. *She laughs.* That's the ideal profile they'd established. So I truly believe—not in a sentimental way—that my appointment was a movement of the Spirit, a falling in love. It was a surprise for us all.

We all did lots of praying and talking. I was just passing through and had nothing to lose by interviewing. I was their "minority candidate" that they had to interview. So we were all completely honest.

It was an adjustment, coming from a church of sixteen hundred to one of just under two hundred. My friends said, "Why are you downsizing?" But I really think I've found my niche.

Sometimes folks here joke that a bigger church will take me away, but I'm not so sure. In a small church like this you have a relational ministry instead of a program ministry.

We're mostly made up of established empty-nesters here. It's pretty homogeneous. If a church in a big city has fifty lifestyles represented, we have maybe five of those lifestyles. Some people come here from the city and say that they miss the big choir, or the Sunday-school program of seven hundred. But though we look homogeneous, in a way we're not. We're the only church of this denomination in town, so that brings some diversity. They're mostly retired—not white-collar really but not blue-collar either. Really a mix.

People live here because they have a boat. They like to dig clams, go crabbing, catch fish. They like it when their grandkids come to visit. I'm getting used to the fact that if there's a good tide, or if it's opening day of a fishing season, folks will take off with their grandkids and miss church. I'm beginning to think that's OK. I believe in a sabbath, but it's not necessarily the traditional one.

*   *   *

Here there's really no expectation that the church will grow. If it grows, that's fine; if not, that's okay too. Jesus said "Feed my sheep"; he didn't say "Count my sheep." So often people feel counted but not fed. They go away hungry. People smell it when you're counting them. *She laughs.*

A lot of us clergypeople get stressed about the numbers thing. Here we try to set nonnumerical goals. The goals are to find a challenge. They don't want graphs and charts and demographic profiles.

Deep in my heart, though, I guess we have this nagging feeling that we're not as good as a bigger church. We get these Sunday-school materials that say, "Divide your fourth grade into four groups." Right! We might have two kids in the fourth grade.

Being single is interesting. They joked after they hired me that they were going to form a PSSC—Pastor's Spouse Search Committee.

They figured that I might stay longer if I was married.

I'm not sure, though. The tendency for workaholism is definitely there. Being single, I'm more available. I get more dinner invitations. Sometimes I'll drop by someone's house on business, and they'll just tell me to stick around for supper. It's a lot easier to feed a single pastor than a pastor, spouse and children.

Sometimes I worry that my style might change if I married.

Dating's not really a problem. People are used to seeing me out in this rather small community with lots of different kinds of people, so it's not assumed that I'm on a date. When I date, I date privately, out of town.

Telling someone right off that I'm a pastor can be a bit of a downer. Sometimes I fudge a little and say I'm in life insurance. If I say I'm a pastor, there's two things that happen. Either the guy tells me he hates the church, left it at fifteen because it ruined his life, or he gets wide-eyed and tells me he's never met a woman minister. "What do I call you? Pastor? Reverend?" I tell him my name will be fine.

As far as social life goes, though, I must say that I've never had so many friends. We go into the city to the opera, to a movie. They introduce me as a friend, not as their pastor, so then I'm allowed to have an evening out. Otherwise, someone will say, "Well, you won't like me, I drink," or something like that. Then as I get to know the people and establish some common ground, I can tell them I'm a pastor and it's fine.

We clergy have a big identity crisis in today's society. We're not sure what our role is. At one time we were the most educated people in the community. We had authority to tell people what to do. People gave the pastor free medical and dental care, a free suit. We had a clearly defined niche. Now no one knows where we fit. I preach to people who are way better educated than me—and to some folks who can't read or write.

Americans have been deeply betrayed by religion, politics and business. They're very suspicious of us, and rightly so sometimes. Now people are just as happy to get married by a judge, so the clergy doesn't have a hold on them, but one gift of modern times is that we get to be comfortable in our own skin. I'm not defined by my authority, but by who I am.

*   *   *

There are two challenges that I like to keep thinking about, that help me to know if this is a healthy calling: am I being authentic in my pastoral role, and does this congregation make me a better person? Sometimes pastors and congregations get mismatched, and they have to be phony. A pastoral call should make the *pastor* a better person, not just the *pastored.*

In a big church you are judged as an administrator. Can she run a program? Can she develop and stick to a budget? They don't ask whether she can conduct a funeral or preach a sermon.

Pastors are practitioners of the conceptual disciplines, and that's hard to quantify. Our job is really to promote love, justice, God's will, accountability . . . We live our lives in the gray area that can't be explained on a spreadsheet.

The neighborhood church is going the way of the neighborhood grocery store. Now people go to Costco, or Safeway, where they have a bigger selection and more choices.

As I see all the changes in society and in the church, I have to ask, What am I paid to do? If you ask me, I'll say, "Pray, preach, do pastoral discipline." If you were to ask the congregation, they'd probably say, "Be active in the community, be a guest at different organizations."

There was a national survey on this topic among deacons. They all disagreed, but the three areas that came up most often were worship, pastoral care and emergency visitation.

That's a fair amount of shifting gears, and sometimes you dress differently for the different tasks. I wear a collar when I do a funeral for a nonchurch family. It makes them feel comfortable. Also when I go to the hospital in the city. If I just say I'm the pastor, they look at me like "Yeah, right." If I have a collar on, they feel it's okay to let me visit. I'm personally more comfortable being called by my first name, but sometimes establishing a pastoral presence is helpful.

I wear a robe when I preach. According to the dictates of fashion, a man can wear the same black or blue suit every week, but a woman can't. It would become a distraction to some of the people, like wearing the same dress to every party. So I wear the robe. It helps people focus on Jesus and the gospel rather than what I'm wearing.

Sometimes I've found that pastors who don't wear a robe have "personality churches." They establish authority through their own personality. I think that everything should point away from the person and to the cross.

In my big-city church I was probably making forty thousand dollars less than the head pastor, but I was expected to dress just as well. In that church, and in many others, you learn to dress for success. So when I came here I was wearing my suits and those little silk scarfs. Finally, after a service, someone came up to me and said, "What are you trying to prove, dressing up like that?"

Now I dress more casually. If we're going to be moving boxes around, I'll come to work in jeans.

* * *

What do I like best about this job? I have the honor to be present in a pastoral way at births, deaths and other really important times.

I believe in the priesthood of all believers, but my vows make me responsible for the institutional church. That means that I can't just go off on my own. My theology is more liberal than that of most of my congregation, but it's not right for me to try to ram that down their throats.

The national church needs to build trust, and I am a part of that process. Pastorally it's not my task to say to a person, "This is what you must believe on this issue." If a person wants to make abortion or refugees or war the issue upon which our salvation hinges, it's better for me to ask, in a pastoral way, "Why is this the issue for you?"

Sometimes the national church will get a lot of bad publicity, such as when they commissioned a study on sexuality a while back. The committee's report made a lot of folks pretty mad. We clergy need to explain the process. This is a *report,* not an encyclical.

As Christians we need to see what the Scriptures say, and when that's not clear, we need to ask, Does this lead to life or death?

The church does need to reevaluate its stand on issues of sexuality, but I have souls in my flock who are at least a decade away from even wanting to hear about human sexuality.

The kingdom is not built on issues. My dad is a hawk, and during the Vietnam War we belonged to a church that didn't grow because of some divisive stands the national church made. Even now, there are people who still feel betrayed by some of those things from twenty years ago.

Good Christians are going to disagree on a lot of life-and-death issues. The church can be the place where we stay together as we struggle through those issues. My personal view on abortion is not the issue. The issue is the kingdom, and I should not use my position as pastor to make it a divisive issue in the congregation.

I was afraid that the Persian Gulf War was going to be a divisive issue. Fortunately, it was over so soon that the people didn't fall into two camps. I was glad that the aftermath of that war didn't get ugly like the years after Vietnam.

There are churches that are built on issues, and we need pastors who are on the cutting edges of issues, but a single issue is never the whole gospel. I respect a lot of the "single-issue" churches. I don't know of any one of them that's not drawn together by the pain of injustice and a real desire to bring healing and justice.

If you look at the Metropolitan Church, which ministers to homosexuals, many of those people are drawn there because they are Christians whose churches denied their pain. The single-issue churches are responding to pain, but they also draw people whose agenda is that issue, not the kingdom and the gospel.

When you talk issues, you really mess with people's worldview. A pastor has to be sensitive to this. You can't just tell people, "Here's the word on refugees, or abortion, or homosexuality." Maybe at some time in the future we'll understand these issues better, and we will change our thinking, but right now I have to say on homosexuality, for instance, that the Scriptures seem to recognize heterosexual relations within marriage as the only appropriate sexuality for Christians. That shouldn't keep me from responding to the pain of homosexual Christians, though.

We had an issue in the local schools based on some textbooks that some people considered New Age. I think that the books were at least influenced by New Age philosophy, but I hesitated to get too involved on the level of being for or against the books. It was pretty mean-spirited on both sides at times. It's not healthy to define yourself by your enemies.

A Career
Is Not the Same
as a Calling
30

He's a scholarly, bookish grandfather who recently "retired" at the age of seventy-two. Although he's given up his suburban parish, he assists regularly at a church in the city. We meet in his home, which contains many pictures of children and grandchildren. There's a shot of him in a leather football helmet, taken at a big Ivy League game. A huge black dog snoozes on a throw rug.

He comes across as a man deeply at peace with himself. He's patient, gracious and charming, yet his passion for ideas surfaces again and again, sharpening the timbre of his voice and igniting a spark in his eyes.

*   *   *

*R*eally, my life in the ministry has been pretty stress-free. I fought the big spiritual battles before I entered the ministry. I felt a great disillusionment with the world after coming out of college. My father was a clergyman, and I knew about the stress and horrors of the job. We talked, and he suggested I go to seminary for one year, without any strings attached. A lot of fellows go to seminary with their tuition paid by a church or parish. That makes it hard to change your mind if you don't really feel the call. My father paid my way so that I would not be obligated to go on if it seemed wrong to do so. It was very gracious of him, because it allowed me to expose myself to the discipline without feeling pressured one way or another. There is a great distinction between a career and a calling.

I graduated from an Ivy League university, and I can see in what happened the plan of God. A friend of mine, who was on the football team with me, came from a very wealthy family. His parents intervened with the Cunard steamship lines, so that he got a summer job serving on what they called the North Cape Cruise. He suggested that I come with him to apply. They looked at both of us, and then I was offered a job as a steward. This was before I entered the seminary.

The cruise was rather casually organized, not like today where every moment is planned out. Part of my job was to see that the young women, who vastly outnumbered the young men, were danced with and taken care of.

I embarked on this rather glamorous life and got a taste of what my wealthier college chums would be doing in their lives. We were always invited to drinks and caviar. It was all quite grand.

But it was also quite unrealistic, and I soon tired of it. I got off at Cherbourg and went to Munich in my jeans—quite a change from the tux I wore on the ship. I thought to myself that I'd experienced a life in which I was forced to be kind and courteous, but it was very phony.

In Germany—this was in the thirties—I saw that in contrast to England, where everyone was so poor, people were fat and well fed. English children all seemed to have rotten teeth, but the Germans were healthy. They were full of great enthusiasm, singing and marching. But I wondered to myself what was happening, because it was all very unsettling.

I went to an art exhibit, but it wasn't art; it was all propaganda, designed to perpetuate Nazi myths about the purity of races and such. The true nature and the falsity were beginning to show through. I saw that outward prosperity could be linked with terrible evil and spiritual decay.

I came back first-class on the *Queen Mary*, without a cent to my name. I was put in first class because the other cabins were full. I worked my way back, of course. The whole experience showed me the things I *didn't* want out of life. As a result, when I got to seminary

I was ready to study. I had a different attitude because of what I had seen. I wanted spiritual truth, not just prosperity.

I felt unusual in seminary, because so many of the other fellows hadn't really been anywhere. Part of conversion, though, is to view others through the Incarnation, and I tried to do that.

In seminary I had one great teacher. He was ahead of his time in that he taught situational ethics in the framework of the kingdom. He taught that there were few specifics in the Christian life. There *are* specifics—things like marriage are quite concrete—but it's not just a big list of inflexible codes and laws. I learned that there are some things that are concrete and many things that are hard to discern.

My belief in the sanctity of Christian marriage is still a very strong part of my ministry. I can't feel right about just marrying someone as though I were a civil servant. I have to believe that it's a sacramental, Christian marriage. Sometimes if I feel particularly uneasy about two people who want to be married, I'll extract myself from the situation. In this day and age, you can't, as a minister, tell people they may not be married. That's no longer part of our role.

If I'm just a bit uneasy about the couple, that's different. That's where grace comes in. No couple is perfect, or perfectly suited to one another. But if they seek a Christian marriage, I work with them.

One of the most specific areas in Scripture is the sanctity, permanence and dignity of marriage. If the people don't believe this way I can't officiate, and I use all the tact and skill I can muster. If they or their parents are members of the parish, it's hard to just tell them no in a blunt or potentially hurtful way. I would hope that by explaining why I can't officiate it might challenge them to think in a constructive way about marriage.

Sometimes it's better to speak rhetorically. I might say to them, "I could break the laws of my church and marry you, but would you put me in that position?" Young people seem to understand and aren't offended, but often the parents, if they're members of the church, are offended. The young people generally prevail over the parents, though.

*   *   *

I've had a few friends who are also in the ministry. I get along well with clergymen who are in ministry, but as soon as I detect careerism it turns me off.

You need spiritual gifts to be successful in ministry. A list of goodies doesn't mean you have a calling. Before I accepted the call, I threw out the list of positive reasons to enter the ministry, and then I threw out the lists of negatives—the smallness, pettiness, legalism, democracy-equals-Christianity, poor thinking, poor living, sentimentality. After this I was exhausted, and God spoke. A true calling bears a sacramental imprint.

When I meet a clergyman who is uncomfortable talking about spiritual things, who just wants to talk about what the diocese is doing, I get uncomfortable.

I've had many associates during my ministry, but one really stands out. When I interviewed him, we spent two days discussing the gospel, the Bible, prayer, healing. It was wonderful. We never discussed salary. He never asked, "What can you offer me?" He was the most wonderful, godly man. Our association, which lasted several years, was marked by joy and a sense of that sacramental imprint.

*   *   *

I always wear clericals. I just said early on, "OK, I'm a priest, so why not accept it?" I still foul up, but this issue was settled a long time ago: I'm a priest, and I should be no different inside or outside the church.

Sometimes I'll be at a social function, a ball game or something, and people will want me to counsel with them. It has bothered me sometimes, but not so that I was in a state of rebellion over it. I'm a priest and that's what I do.

One of my worst mistakes in that area was with my old college buddies at a reunion. I thought, "Oh, good. I can just have a great time with people I really like," so I just let loose and had a great time. I didn't go out drinking or carousing, nothing that I wouldn't ordinarily do, but I really let down my guard. My wife told me later that I don't ever laugh the way I laughed with those fellows.

But I wanted to have a good time, and I didn't stop to talk to a fellow who really needed me. I truly regret that now, because I'm on this earth to be a priest and I missed a chance to help someone.

*   *   *

Sometimes I get away, just by myself, to read, pray and sleep. I try to protect my day off, but I also try to remember that being available when I'm needed is part of my calling. I try to follow the sabbath. For me it's not a Sunday sabbath, because that's when we're most busy, but a day of rest, prayer, reflection and meditation.

I've tried to read books on preaching but they don't really help me. I'm not a great preacher, so I have to be satisfied with what I can do.

I'm most happy being in the right place at the right time—I stop in at the hospital, and there is somebody who needs me. I like to be available for people. I live close to the church, but that's never been a problem. Again, it's part of the calling.

Lately, the seminaries have been turning out CEOs. There's a lack of spirituality in seminary teaching. It's becoming more career-oriented. You try to become dean of the seminary, and then a bishop.

I talked to a seminary dean who was looking for a good Old Testament teacher. He interviewed a fellow at the cathedral who seemed to fit the bill perfectly. They talked, and then the Old Testament man said, "It sounds interesting, but just last week they gave me a raise!"

Life and
Death in the
City

31

In this blue-collar city whose timber- and mining-related industries have fallen on hard times lately, the African-American community has been plagued by an increase in violent crime. The murderous Crips and Blood gangs from L.A. have established a foothold in the streets, and even in the schools. The media paint a grim picture of drive-by shootings and crack houses.

In one of the most celebrated news stories, soldiers from a nearby army base exchanged over three hundred rounds with drug dealers in a fierce gun battle that miraculously left no dead.

As I arrive for the interview, I am surprised to find a calm-looking street lined with modest homes and businesses. The TV news crews focus on boarded-up houses and littered streets, but my first impression is of a pleasant, friendly neighborhood. His church building is fairly new and well kept up.

I'm escorted to the pastor's study, where I meet a soft-spoken black man in his forties. His manner is like that of a college professor during an office-hours conference. I have interrupted his morning coffee break, and the secretary brings me a cup.

Some interviews are intense. Some begin stiffly. He is casual, friendly and interested in my book. We talk about the book for a while, and then he begins to talk about the life of a pastor. We turn to the subject of being an example in a community with some big problems.

*   *   *

*I*t's not easy to be a pastor. One thing people don't really think about is that pastors are sinners, but they are called out to do a special job. We weren't born pastors. You do have to project a certain image, though.

That's OK, though. We're supposed to be called out to teach and preach to others to follow in the ways of the Lord.

It's especially hard on the wives. I bought my wife a book a while back called *Help! I'm a Pastor's Wife!* That says it pretty well. Your life is looked at in a different way. The kids too.

When my son was nine or ten, the kids at school teased him. Because he was a preacher's kid, he couldn't fight back. They thought so, anyway! Well, he proved he could fight. He shouldn't be picked on just because he's my son. He defended himself just like anyone else. He's a teenager now.

My wife has a problem with all the moving. I'm an itinerant minister. My bishop assigns me to churches that don't have a permanent pastor, so I move around a lot. One of the big drawbacks is that I don't stay long in one place, so I don't get to know people as closely as I might.

So who do I tell my own problems to? If it weren't for my wife, I'd be lost. I just don't get to know people well enough that I can share my heart. I deal with sorrow and death a lot, and it gets pretty heavy to bear.

Last week I was called to the hospital by the family of a nine-year-old boy who was on life support. He had meningitis, and there was no hope. The family decided to pull the plug, so I sat there with them and watched him die. They shut off the machines, but it took him a while to die. There was nothing physical that we could do. We just watched him slip away. Nine is too young, and it broke my heart.

A while ago one of my musicians was dying of AIDS. I watched him die too. Yesterday I watched while an elderly lady was taken off life support. It makes you want to go to the top of a mountain and scream. I hate going to the hospital.

I conduct funerals for people in and out of the church. Even for kids I don't know—boys in the gangs, a lot of them. Everyone has high expectations of the church, even those who mock the church. They might ridicule the church as they cruise around with their gangs, but when their friends get killed they want the church. That's okay. It's what we're here for. But it's hard to watch kids ruin their lives and finally come to the church in a coffin. You want to have a chance with them while they're still alive. When you can help them to know the Lord.

I always try to be prayed up. I'm not always going to get what the Lord wants me to get, but if I'm prayed up I'll get closer to his will than if I just go charging around on my own.

During a gang funeral I saw a boy sitting in the back. The funeral was for a young man, a teenager, who'd been shot by some other kids. Those are hard funerals to do, because it seems like such a tragic, hopeless waste. Well, this boy was having a real hard time. He was crying, and he'd get overcome with grief and just get up and leave. In a few moments he'd come back, then he'd lose control and get up and leave again.

I was able to get to him after the service. I asked him about his life, his gang, the death of the young fellow in the casket they'd just carried out the door. He was probably not old enough to get a driver's license, but he was talking about drugs and crime and guns—how somebody was gonna pay for killing his friend. He was living in a whole different world. I said, "Are you comfortable with your life, the way it's going?" He said *"No!"* A big no.

I talked to him about the Lord. He listened, I think, but he was so full of hate and anger and sorrow. I invited him to come to church, but I don't know if I'll ever see him again. Maybe I'll help bury *him* next week. I hope not.

All that dying and sorrow can really get you down, but on the other hand I love to preach the gospel. I love to see people change. A good pastor is always concerned. You can't just preach like you're doing a job. Sometimes I feel that maybe I'm preaching in vain, because I see that people need the Lord and they don't respond.

Change can happen in different ways, though. It may happen piece by piece. Maybe my preaching is just one little part of it, but God is working on that person and he has a plan. I've just done a little tiny part of the preaching that's gonna change that person.

Down South I preached in a church where a man who'd been a church member over forty years, and an officer of the church for over thirty years, accepted the invitation to come down and meet Jesus. He wanted to be saved. I was shocked! But all that time he'd been going to church, listening, and it took that long for him to realize that he was lost. Two weeks later he died.

So in spite of the hospital visits where I watch someone die, in spite of burying kids who've been shot, I love being a preacher. I love to preach. Even when people seem to ignore it. I love being around people, even in their pain and loss. That's part of the calling, so I wouldn't try to avoid it.

If there was something that would just make you throw in the towel and go do something else, what would it be?

Board meetings! Dealing with church folks about the running of the church business. That's funny. You know, it never crossed my mind in all these years to quit and do something else until you mentioned it just now. Yeah, board meetings. People think they know how to run the church, but they just don't. Some folks act all sanctified on Sunday, but they raise a pound of hell come board meeting.

My toughest job is writing sermons. For some that comes easy, but not for me. I spend maybe twenty or twenty-two hours a week thinking, praying, meditating, studying—most of all, waiting on the Holy Spirit to give me the right thing to say.

This is my fourth church in fifteen years. My predecessor was here seven and a half years, and his last two years were the worst. The bishop sent me here and moved him elsewhere. The church was losing members and just about to die. We've gained 450 new members since 1988. Before, I knew everyone's name. Now I have to be careful. I was shaking hands in the foyer, and I told a lady how nice it was that she came to visit us. She said, "Pastor! I'm a member!" But we have eight hundred members now.

We're seeing more young people. Couples in their twenties who are eager to hear the Word. We had over twenty young adults visit this last Sunday. Usually people drop out in their twenties. I did. And they come back later, in their thirties, when their kids are growing up.

Why this turnaround in your church? Why the influx of younger people?

People are not dull anymore. They lead exciting lives, and they need an exciting church. People have to believe that what's happening in church is important. It's not like they have nothing to do but come on Sunday and sit there while somebody goes on and on about nothing.

As a pastor you have to see what's changing and meet those changes. Even in techniques. We have computers, faxes. A lot of things that I don't know how to fully utilize.

You have to pray that the Lord will call people to do those things. I have six assistant ministers, a secretary and an assistant secretary.

We have class leaders whose job it is to call and see what the church can do for new folks. If pastors think people just come to hear them preach, they're sadly mistaken.

But the preacher's got to preach. Not everybody in church is going to heaven. You have to preach it. Just having your name on the rolls won't get you into heaven.

* * *

If you want to be a preacher, you have to realize that some things are going to be hard, like dealing with death. There's things you can't explain when people really need an explanation.

And board meetings! But you can't really learn that except by experience. You have to learn that you can't get everything you want.

Keep the peace, but also learn not to back down.

No Students
or Shoppers
32

He's a baby boomer, a child of the sixties, whose latest book deals with being an outsider in the denominational clique. Known for his unorthodox orthodoxy, he's a bit of an anomaly in a mainline denomination whose churches are getting older and smaller. Faced with the pressure to conform to denominational stereotypes, he is one of the few who have just said no.

We meet shortly after he accepts a call to serve as senior pastor in a large church in another state. He leaves one of the largest, fastest-growing, most evangelical churches in his denomination, where he has served in a multistaff pastorate.

*   *   *

I began looking for a senior pastorate when my senior pastor left. He was a mentor to me, and I had made a commitment to stay here as long as he was around. I still like this place, and I'm not walking out, nothing like that.

It came down to my being seriously considered by three big churches in the Midwest and West. When they expressed interest, I sent them each a copy of my book, since it pretty much lays out my pastoral philosophy.

The church I'm going to said yes. That was what they were looking for. Another church flew me out for an interview, then a couple of the elders said, "We have studied your book and we have some serious concerns." So why did they fly me out for an interview?

The interview process is pretty educational. You see pretty clearly what people think a pastor is. Pastors are like women. They're placed up on a pedestal so that you don't have to take them seriously. You can admire them from afar without getting close. You don't have to be honest with them, and they'd better not be honest with you.

I refuse to be on a pedestal, and when you get off that pedestal the rules change. That's the only way I can serve as a pastor. I allowed myself to get put on the pedestal in my first church, before I came here. I was dying in a pile!

Sometimes the pedestal syndrome is just funny. Our new senior pastor is rather short, which is unusual for a senior pastor, since we're kind of like celebrities. Every senior pastor in our denomination is tall, with a full head of hair. Tony Campolo would never be hired in our group.

One day I mentioned to the new senior pastor that he should turn on the light in the pulpit so that the congregation could see him. It's kind of a stupid lighting system. It shines down on the pages and then reflects up on your face. Well, he said he didn't like the light.

A few more weeks went by, but he didn't want the light. We told him that people could not see his face in church. "It gets between me and the people," he insisted.

Then I realized. It shines in his eyes. "I'm short," he said, like it was a sin or something.

I explained that the pulpit was adjustable, and we could raise the platform on which he stood. We did, and the next week we could see his face. Then the following week another pastor who is about six-foot-four preached, and it looked really goofy. His text was down by his knees, and the light shone up on his stomach. We busted a gut over that one.

But you know, once a famous preacher from the seminary was coming to town and I was his host. Each time he called me, he asked when he could come by and see the pulpit. I said that the pulpit was fine and not to worry, and just brushed him off. After the sixth call he finally said, "Well, I'm kind of short, and we might have to stack some hymnals up for me to stand on." He just couldn't come out and say he was short. So I told him it was adjustable and we'd raise it up. No problem.

*   *   *

Anyway, this church that called me had it down to me and another guy. The other guy is great. I know him, and I respect and like him. But they told me that the final reason they called me was because he was "Reverend" and I was "Bob." I was glad to hear that, because I don't want to have to be self-conscious about everything. I can't work that way.

The other church that interviewed me had some pretty serious problems. When I talked to their people on the phone, before the interview, I asked about the health of the church. Were there any battles, schisms, etc.? They said, rather demurely, "Well, there have been some problems."

I'll say! When I stepped off the plane, I picked up a local paper. The banner headline on the front page said: "Local church rocked by sex scandal!" They had "some problems" all right.

Were they going to tell you about the scandal?

That's the first thing I asked them. They said they were, but they wanted to be discreet. Discreet! With a banner headline, television news stories . . . It was the big story in town, and they were going to be *discreet?*

They were in pretty deep denial. I think they were hoping to just send the guy off to another pastorate and pronounce him healed. He had some profound problems, though. He'd had many, many affairs with women in the church. That kind of deception can indicate that something's very wrong in the congregation and the elder board.

Is sexual abuse as widespread in the ministry as the media would have us believe?

Actually, the guy that preceded my mentor at this church was defrocked. He'd had over two hundred affairs, and finally a church secretary blew the whistle on him. That left a pretty unhappy bunch of campers for the new pastor to minister to. Surprisingly, not many people know about it now. I guess they were more uptight about letting people know back then. It makes you feel for the people that left the church out of hurt and betrayal. Who pastored them?

It seems that there are a lot of those kinds of issues that blindside pastors. A number of pastors have complained that seminary doesn't teach them much about the infighting and politics that go on in churches.

I was asked to teach a seminar at my seminary called "What They Never Teach in Seminary." I talked about the nitty-gritty. There's so much that is vacuous in seminary. It's not really about pastoring. How do we think about families that fight? How do we deal with adultery and deception? There's a conspiracy against talking about the real issues, just like in our church. They haven't talked about that pastor who years and years ago caused people to stumble in their faith. How do we minister to those hurts? How do we learn from what happened?

One of the seminary professors resented what I said. He told me that seminary was not a trade school for pastors; it was a think tank for theologians.

Theologians are needed, but only to support and encourage the church. They're not much use if they just sit around arguing arcane points with one another. Then they just become another group of "professionals" with a vested interest in the status quo.

Fear drives us. We spend so much time worrying about our image, our pensions. When you look at the church in the book of Acts and see what we've become—this cautious status-quo club—it makes you weep.

I used to hope that when the current generation of pastors retired and died—that sounds terrible—a new generation would come into the pulpit and shake things up, get away from being a denomination and be a church.

It sounds like you don't hold much hope for that now.

It sure doesn't look promising. I helped form a consortium of new pastors who wanted to move the church into a more active, evangelistic, discipling stance. We were mostly younger guys. When I say "younger," I mean people in their thirties and forties.

Most of the senior pastors are now in their sixties. They went through the Depression, World War II and Korea. The McCarthy era and the Cold War are their reference points. Our reality, on the other hand, began with the sixties—Vietnam and the civil rights movement.

When we got together a while ago, I was so depressed. My peers had become churchmen. They had taken on all the traits of the older generation—the desire to grease the wheels of the organization. All of the vision was gone and replaced with programs.

What does this mean for the future?

In our denomination, the senior pastors of all the megachurches will retire in three to five years. But there aren't any pastors in their fifties. In the sixties, the people who went into seminary came out as counselors and social workers, or they became entrenched bureaucrats. They work in the church headquarters and church organizations, but they can't stay in the pulpits. Quite a lot of them just plain lost their faith, in all the relativism and modernism of the age.

There was a group of clergymen from our denomination in town who were all counselors. They hadn't been in a pulpit in years. They were very liberal in their theology, but they wanted to remain ordained. They perceived me as a sort of fellow traveler, so they came to me and asked me what I thought they should do. I told them that the only reason they were remaining in the denomination was for the retirement program. They didn't believe the Word, so they were just prostitutes.

How did they respond to that?

Not well. I was no longer their fellow traveler. I told them to go join the Unitarians. That's where they really belonged.

The main task of a pastor—at least in my opinion—is not to teach or to counsel, but to remind God's people who they are, where they've been and where they're going. I'm like a Post-It. That's what I told those guys. The job of a pastor is to build people. You can't do that if you don't believe in the gospel. It involves church discipline and holding to the historical faith.

Some pastors say that their flocks are pretty resistant to church discipline. People just threaten that they'll go elsewhere if the church tries to discipline them.

I keep a photocopied list of dead churches that I give to those people.

Really?

Yes. I just say, here's where you'll be welcome. Your adultery, or whatever, won't be a problem. I knew a pastor—he'd been a friend of mine—who had a string of affairs. He moved to a denomination where that wasn't perceived as a problem. Now he can be a pastor and commit adultery with women in the church.

How would you go about finding pastors who won't just become professional clergypeople? How do you get to seminarians before they become co-opted?

It has to start before that. Right now, we just wait for someone to step up to the bat, and then we train them. But we have to look at the reasons people enter seminary. Sometimes it's people who have no job prospects, so they think, "Hey! I could go to seminary." Sometimes it's people who had a rough life and their pastor was nice to them. So they want to be pastors too.

I've been involved in a project with a seminary and a college in which we train pastors as they serve in the congregations. That way, they apply what they are learning to what they are doing. And they come to class with lots of good questions. They don't just spend years preparing for a job that exists only in their own minds.

We need to recruit people in midcareer. People who have a heart for Jesus and for people. We need to find them, and then support them. Mature people who have made it in the world and are ready for a move. Then the church could raise up a new generation of pastors. We need to seek them out and ask what we can do to make it happen.

You were fairly young when you took your first pulpit. Did that experience lead you to regret going in so young?

I got a first-class education in American religion at that church. Their attitude was "Let's get this young longhair with wire-rim glasses to preach, and the church will grow." I was so stupid that I believed it. I was going to bring the younger generation in.

The church had once had about a thousand members. The sanctuary was small, so they put folding chairs out on the patio and ran four services. They owned five acres of land in a growing community.

They'd had only two pastors in about ninety years. One died in office, and the other retired. Then my predecessor came in, and the place started to shrink during his ten-year tenure. When I arrived, the church was down to 110 members and sinking fast.

I couldn't figure out why things were so dead, so finally I called the previous pastor just to chat and see if I could get a handle on the situation.

I asked him how it was going in his new church. He said, "Well, I feel sort of uneasy. I don't really like large churches." His new church was about a thousand. He said, "I like a smaller church, where I know everybody." This is the guy who'd walked my church down from a thousand to two hundred! He just went into a big church and brought it down to a comfortable size. He put up walls that kept people out.

So was it really all his fault?

Not entirely. But his attitude began to shape the place. When you get a church in a posture, the people who agree stick around and the others drift off. I got handed the people who chose to stay there. The ones who liked it that way.

After two years of being frustrated by a mandate to bring people in and a practice of keeping them out, I asked my wife, "Have you noticed that everybody here is pretty happy?"

"Everybody but us," she said. "They want it this way." That's when we left and came here.

Now the church is a bit smaller and has a caretaker pastor. They're selling off property to pay their bills.

Changing the subject a bit, your denomination has had its share of pronouncements that have angered more orthodox, evangelical follow-ers. How do you deal with things on the denominational level that you see as unbiblical?

Never confuse the national church with the kingdom of God. The organization is there to help the congregations within the denomination. But when you get a big denomination like ours, the national office takes on a life of its own. The church and the denomination will always exist in tension. It's the same with individual churches. They always run the risk of becoming ends in themselves.

My wife and I went back East once, so we decided to visit one of the historic cathedral churches of our denomination. We wanted to sit in the middle. But a few minutes later I felt a tap-tap-tap on my shoulder and an old lady said, "Excuse me. You're in my seat!"

I just smiled and said, "Well, this will give you a chance to meet someone new," and I held out my hand. She didn't take it. She just waited for me to move. Which I did not do.

It was a crazy place. The ushers were wearing—and I'm not making this up—tuxedos and white gloves. Yes! They just sort of whooshed us in, like water going through a chute, and when it was over they whooshed us out and closed the doors. We "did" church, but we didn't meet anyone except the lady whose seat we took. That church is getting smaller and older each year. No wonder! What young person is going to go there?

It's the same in this city. One of our churches here used to have fifteen thousand members. Now it's down to about two hundred old people in a sanctuary that holds fifteen hundred.

Why is it all old people?

It's an attitude. I've even seen churches that have signs that say, "No Single Adults."

You must be making this up!

Nope. Young, single adults threaten the status quo. People will tell you that it's about lifestyle, ethics, theology, whatever. But what's at the root of most church hassles is power. People want power. If new, younger people come in, they might want to share the power. So we keep them out.

Sometimes it's just plain bullheadedness, too. *He laughs.* Our church is situated between a university and a shopping district. Parking is very scarce, so when we built our parking garage they put a sign up over the garage entrance that says, "No Students or Shoppers." But you can't see the parking entrance, and the sign is right under the sign with the name of the church. It looks like it says, "No Shoppers or Students Need Apply"!

Doesn't that sign face the university dorms across the street?

Yes! So at the church meeting we said, "Let's take it down." But the elders, well, they weren't so sure. Finally, the campus ministry pastor went out there with duct tape and covered up the "students" part. He was beside himself!

Some people would see that as an act of rebellion.

You bet. That's what you have to do as a pastor. You have to run a guerrilla ministry. You have to get to the point where you don't need the organization and make sure that you don't need your job. The organization should serve the ministry, not the other way around.

Imagine hiring a talented pastor to reach out to the university students and then putting up a sign that says, "No Students or Shoppers." Right! And then we expect the students to come in droves!

That sign was an honest mistake. But it became wrong when they wouldn't take it down. If you ever go into a church session and ask for something, the answer will probably be no.

So you just do what you want?

Not what you want. What you must do. You pray and search the Scriptures, then you do it. But don't make it an issue of contention or ego. If you get caught breaking the rules, you apologize.

Afterword

Now that we have heard what pastors say off the record, how shall we treat our pastors? Or what, then, is their legitimate role? The Scriptures give broad guidelines, but not a detailed job description.

Much depends on how we define our congregations. If a congregation sees itself as a nonprofit charitable organization, it may want a CEO. On the other end of the continuum, a church that sees itself as a big family may expect its pastor to be a parent figure who visits each member on a regular basis. A church primarily interested in evangelism may expect the pastor to lead community outreaches and preach salvation every week.

Most churches draw from various models, so that pastors are expected to fulfill several different, sometimes contradictory roles. Pastors who have a clear understanding of what is expected tend to be the most secure and emotionally approachable, while those whose jobs are too big for them may become defensive and aloof.

But it is not the pastor who should communicate the job description to the congregation. Deacons and elders must make it clear to the congregation what is and what is not expected of the pastor. If church members criticize the pastor for something that is not part of the job description, the elders and deacons should come to the pastor's defense.

Many of the pastors I interviewed had served in churches where every church member had in mind a different job description for the pastor. When no one speaks with authority on the pastor's true role, the pastor has to adapt with each new criticism. A pastor who has to keep piling on new tasks to avoid criticism will not last long. A church is, for better or for worse, an organization, and no one person can run every facet of an organization. Pastors who are expected to do everything will burn out.

But Christ didn't come to sustain organizations. The church is the bride of Christ. The central metaphor is one of marriage and family, and the basic guidelines for a healthy family apply to a healthy church. Families that encourage, uphold and cherish one another are the ones that prosper. Those that expect perfection tend to become hollow façades.

One pastor told me that he appreciated getting a card or note from a parishioner, especially during tough times. Others said that they appreciated being given the chance to be "off-duty" sometimes. All appreciated having friends in the congregation who would let them be themselves.

All of us come to Christ, and to the church, with many needs. Sometimes we forget that our pastors have the same needs as we do. If we truly believe in our pastor's calling, we must also accept that he or she is a needy, sinful person just like us. Like the patriarchs, prophets and apostles, the pastor has a special calling, and like them, the pastor is a fallen creature who needs to be sustained, nurtured and loved.